Rick Steves ®
SNAPSHOT

Milan & the Italian Lakes District

CONTENTS

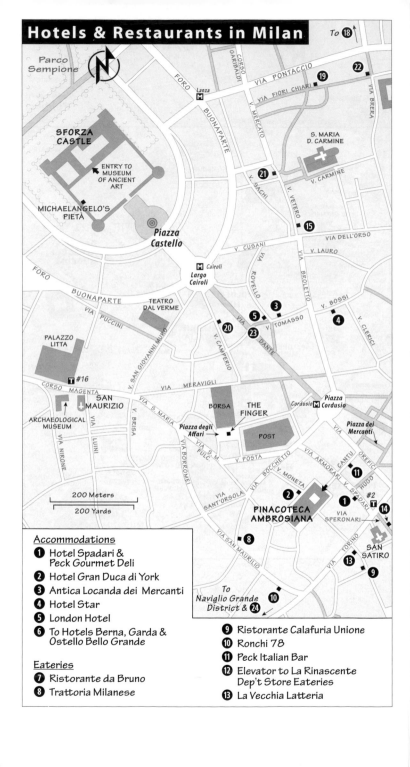

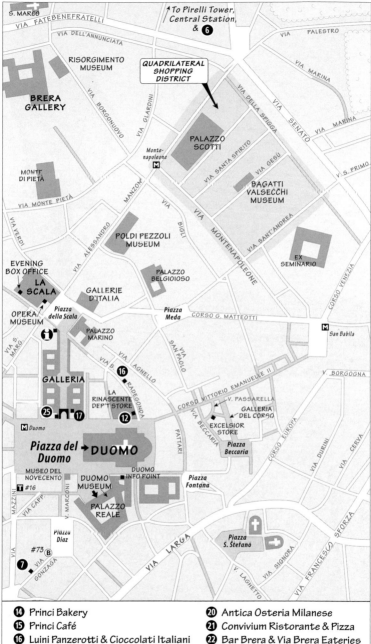

14 Princi Bakery	**20** Antica Osteria Milanese
15 Princi Café	**21** Convivium Ristorante & Pizza
16 Luini Panzerotti & Cioccolati Italiani	**22** Bar Brera & Via Brera Eateries
17 Il Mercato del Duomo	**23** Via Dante Eateries
18 To Eataly	**24** To Naviglio Grande Eateries
19 Via Fiori Chiari Eateries	**25** Bar Camparino

INTRODUCTION

This Snapshot guide, excerpted from my guidebook *Rick Steves Italy*, introduces you to Milan. If Florence represents the Renaissance and Rome equals antiquity, Milan is 21st-century Italy. You can walk on the rooftop of one of Europe's grandest Gothic cathedrals, window-shop in fashionable neighborhoods, visit the world's most famous opera house, and admire a Leonardo masterpiece. Explore the city's grand, glass-domed arcade and stroll along one of Europe's longest pedestrian-only boulevards. Sip an aperitivo at a sidewalk café, and sample Milan's culinary specialties. If you're looking for a sophisticated, smart slice of Italy, you'll find it here.

I also cover the seductively beautiful Italian Lakes District. This region, where Italy meets the Alps, seems heaven-sent for nature lovers. Lake Como offers a mix of accessibility, scenery, and offbeatness with a heady whiff of 19th-century whimsy. Lake Maggiore, though more densely populated and more developed, has exotic garden islands and nearby mountains. The lakes are the place to take a vacation from your vacation, lingering in charming towns such as Varenna or Bellagio. Hop on a lake ferry and glide to dreamy villas, or ride a cable car to pristine alpine meadows.

To help you have the best trip possible, I've included the following topics in this book:

• **Planning Your Time**, with advice on how to make the most of your limited time

• **Orientation,** including tourist information (abbreviated as TI), tips on public transportation, local tour options, and helpful hints

• **Sights** with ratings:

▲▲▲—Don't miss

▲▲—Try hard to see

▲—Worthwhile if you can make it

No rating—Worth knowing about

• **Sleeping** and **Eating**, with good-value recommendations in every price range

• **Connections,** with tips on trains, buses, and driving

Practicalities, near the end of this book, has information on money, staying connected, hotel reservations, transportation, and more, plus Italian survival phrases.

To travel smartly, read this little book in its entirety before you go. It's my hope that this guide will make your trip more meaningful and rewarding. Traveling like a temporary local, you'll get the absolute most out of every mile, minute, and dollar.

Buon viaggio!

Rick Steves

MILAN

Milano

For every church in Rome, there's a bank in Milan. Italy's second city and the capital of the Lombardy region, Milan is a hardworking, style-conscious, time-is-money city of 1.3 million. A melting pot of people and history, Milan's industriousness may come from the Teutonic blood of its original inhabitants, the Lombards, or from its years under Austrian rule. Either way, Milan is modern Italy's center of fashion, industry, banking, TV, publishing, and conventions. It's also a major university town, a train hub, and host to two football (soccer) teams and the nearby Monza Formula One race track. And as home to a prestigious opera house, Milan is one of the touchstones of the world of opera.

Artistically, Milan can't compare with Rome and Florence, but the city does have several unique and noteworthy sights: the Duomo and the Galleria Vittorio Emanuele II arcade, La Scala Opera House, Michelangelo's last *pietà* sculpture (in Sforza Castle), and Leonardo da Vinci's *The Last Supper*.

Founded by the Romans as Mediolanum ("the place in the middle"), by the fourth century A.D. it was the capital of the western half of the Roman Empire, the namesake of Constantine's "Edict of Milan" legalizing Christianity, and home of the powerful early Christian bishop, St. Ambrose.

After some barbarian darkness, medieval Milan became a successful mercantile city, eventually rising to regional prominence under the Visconti and Sforza families. The mammoth cathedral, or Duomo, is a testament to the city's wealth and ambition. By the time of the Renaissance, Milan was nicknamed "the New Athens," and was enough of a cultural center for Leonardo da Vinci to call it home. Then came 400 years of foreign domination (under Spain,

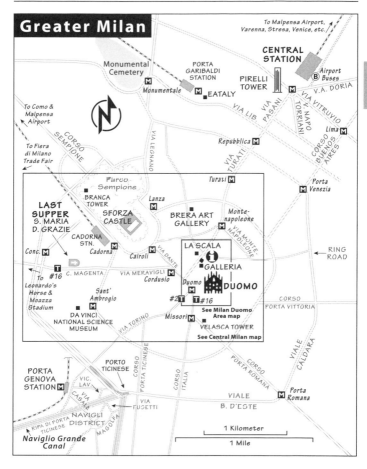

Austria, France, more Austria). Milan was a focal point of the 1848 revolution against Austria and helped lead Italy to unification in 1870. The impressive Galleria Vittorio Emanuele II and La Scala Opera House reflect the sophistication of turn-of-the-century Milan as one of Europe's cultural powerhouses.

Mussolini left a heavy fascist touch on the architecture here (such as the central train station). His excesses also led to the WWII bombing of Milan. But the city rose again. The 1959 Pirelli Tower (the skinny skyscraper in front of the station) was a trendsetter in its day. Today, Milan is people-friendly, with a great transit system and inviting pedestrian zones.

Many tourists come to Italy for the past. But Milan is today's Italy. In this city of refined tastes, window displays are gorgeous, cigarettes are chic, and even the cheese comes gift-wrapped. Yet,

MILAN

thankfully, Milan is no more expensive for tourists than any other Italian city.

For pleasant excursions nearby, consider visiting Lake Como or Lake Maggiore—both are about an hour from Milan by train.

PLANNING YOUR TIME

Milan isn't as charming as Venice or Florence, but it's still a vibrant and vital piece of the Italian puzzle.

With two nights and a full day, you can gain an appreciation for the city and see most major sights. On a short visit, I'd focus on the center. Tour the Duomo, hit any art you like (reserve ahead to see *The Last Supper*), browse elegant shops and the Galleria Vittorio Emanuele II, and try to see an opera. To maximize your time in Milan, use the Metro to get around.

For those with a round-trip flight into Milan: I'd recommend starting your journey softly by going first to Lake Como (one-hour ride to Varenna) or the Cinque Terre (3 hours to Monterosso). Then spend the last night or two of your trip in Milan before flying home.

Monday is a terrible sightseeing day, since many museums are closed (including *The Last Supper*). August is oppressively hot and muggy, and locals who can vacate do, leaving the city quiet. Those visiting in August find that the nightlife is sleepy, and many shops and restaurants are closed.

A Three-Hour Tour: If you're just changing trains at Milan's Centrale station (as, sooner or later, you probably will), consider catching a later train and taking this blitz tour: Check your bag at the station, ride the subway to the Duomo, peruse the square, explore the cathedral's rooftop terraces and interior, drop into the Duomo Museum, have a scenic coffee in the Galleria Vittorio Emanuele II, spin on the floor mosaic of the bull for good luck, maybe see a museum or two (most are within a 10-minute walk of the main square), and return by subway to the station. Art fans could make time for *The Last Supper* (if they've made reservations) and/or Michelangelo's *Pietà* in Sforza Castle (no reservations necessary).

Orientation to Milan

My coverage focuses on the old center. Most sights and hotels listed are within a 15-minute walk of the cathedral (Duomo), which is a straight eight-minute Metro ride from the Centrale train station.

TOURIST INFORMATION

Milan's TI, at the La Scala end of the Galleria Vittorio Emanuele II, isn't worth a special trip (Mon-Fri 9:00-19:00, Sat 9:00-18:00, Sun 10:00-18:00, Metro: Duomo, tel. 02-884-5555, www.turismo.milano.it).

ARRIVAL IN MILAN

By Train: Visitors disembark at one of three major train stations: Milano Centrale, Porta Garibaldi, or Cadorna. Centrale handles most Trenitalia and Italo trains as well as airport buses. Porta Garibaldi receives trains from France and some Trenitalia trains from elsewhere in Italy. Both Centrale and Cadorna are terminals for trains from Malpensa Airport.

At Milano Centrale: This huge, sternly decorated, fascist-built (in 1931) train station is a sight in itself. Notice how the monumental halls and art make you feel small—emphasizing that a powerful state is a good thing. In the front lobby, heroic people celebrate "modern" transportation (circa-1930 ships, trains, and cars) opposite reliefs depicting old-fashioned sailboats and horse carts.

Moving walkways link the station's three main levels: platforms on top, shops on a small mezzanine, and most services at ground level (including pay WCs and ATMs). For baggage check *(Deposito bagagli),* taxis, or buses to the airports, head toward the ground-level exit marked *Piazza Luigi di Savoia.* Outside the station's front entrance, under the atrium, are car-rental offices for Avis, Budget, and Maggiore, and a post office-run ATM. You'll also find escalators down to the Metro and a fourth basement level with a few shops, including a Sapori & Dintorni supermarket. (You can also enter the Metro from inside the station—just follow signs.)

"Centrale" is a misnomer—the Duomo is a 35-minute walk away. But it's a straight shot on the Metro (8 minutes). Buy a €1.50 ticket at a kiosk or from the machines, follow signs for yellow line 3 (direction: San Donato), and go four stops to the Duomo stop. You'll surface facing the cathedral.

To **buy train tickets,** follow blue signs to *Biglietti* and use the Trenitalia or Italo machines for most domestic trips. For international tickets or complicated questions, join the line at the Trenitalia ticket office on the ground floor. There's also an Italo office on the ground floor. Another alternative is the Agenzie 365 travel agency, which sells tickets at several offices in the station: Their 9

Rome vs. Milan: A Classic Squabble

In Italy, the North and South bicker about each other, hurling barbs, quips, and generalizations. All the classic North/South traits can be applied to Milan (the business capital) and Rome (the government and religious capital). Italians like to say that people come to Milan to sin, and they go to Rome to ask for forgiveness.

The Milanesi say the Romans are lazy. Government jobs in Rome come with short hours—made even shorter by multiple coffee breaks, three-hour lunches, chats with colleagues, and phone calls to friends and relatives. Milanesi contend that "Roma *ladrona*" (Rome, the big thief) is a parasite that lives off the taxes of people up North. There's still a strong Milan-based movement promoting secession from the South.

Romans, meanwhile, dismiss the Milanesi as uptight workaholics with nothing else to live for—gray like their foggy city. But Romans do admit that in Milan, job opportunities are better and based on merit. And the Milanesi grudgingly concede the Romans have a gift for enjoying life.

While Rome is more of a family city, Milan is the place for

percent markup can be a reasonable price to skip ticket-office lines, but not if the agency's outlets have lines of their own.

At Milano Cadorna: You're most likely to use this commuter station if you take the Malpensa Express airport train, which uses track 1. The Cadorna Metro station—with a direct connection to the Duomo on Metro red line 1—is directly out front.

At Milano Porta Garibaldi: Some Trenitalia trains and the high-speed TGV from Paris use Porta Garibaldi Station, north of the city center. Porta Garibaldi is on Metro green line 2, two stops from Milano Centrale.

By Car: Leonardo never drove in Milan. Smart guy. Driving here is bad enough to make the €30/day fee for a downtown garage a blessing. If you're driving in Italy, do Milan (and Lake Como) before or after you rent your car, not while you've got it. If you must have a car, use the safe, affordable, well-marked park-and-ride lots at suburban Metro stations such as Cascina Gobba. These are shown on the official Metro map, and full details are at www.atm.it (select English, then "Car Parks," then "Parking Lots").

By Plane: See "Milan Connections" at the end of this chapter.

high-powered singles on the career fast-track. Milanese yuppies mix with each other...not the city's longtime residents. Milan is seen as wary of foreigners and inward-looking, and Rome as fun-loving, tolerant, and friendly. In Milan, bureaucracy (such as social

services) works logically and efficiently, while in Rome, accomplishing even small chores can be exasperating. Everything in Rome—from finding a babysitter to buying a car—is done through friends.

Milanesi find Romans vulgar. The Roman dialect is considered one of the coarsest in the country. Much as they try, Milanesi just can't say "Damn your dead relatives" quite as effectively as the Romans. Still, Milanesi enjoy Roman comedians and love to imitate the accent.

The Milanesi feel that Rome is dirty and Roman traffic nerve-wracking. But despite the craziness, Rome maintains a genuine village feel. People share family news with their neighborhood grocer. Milan lacks people-friendly piazzas, and entertainment comes at a high price. But in Rome, *la dolce vita* is as close as the nearest square, and a full moon is enjoyed by all.

HELPFUL HINTS

Theft Alert: Be on guard. Milan's thieves target tourists, especially at the Centrale train station, getting in and out of the subway, and around the Duomo. They can be dressed as tourists, businessmen, or beggars, or they can be gangs of too-young-to-arrest children. Watch out for ragged people carrying newspapers and cardboard—they'll thrust these at you as a distraction while they pick your pocket. If you're ripped off and plan to file an insurance claim, fill out a report with the police (main police station, "Questura," Via Fatebenefratelli 11, Metro: Turati, open daily 24 hours, tel. 02-62261).

Free Museums: Every Tuesday after 14:00 the Museo del Novecento and Sforza Castle museums are free. They're also free on the first Sunday of the month, as is *The Last Supper* (reservations required; line up at 8:00 that day), the Brera Art Gallery, and the Risorgimento Museum.

Helpful Websites: HelloMilano.com and WantedinMilano.com are decent websites for the latest info on what's happening in the city.

Medical Help: Here are two medical clinics with emergency care facilities (both closed Sat-Sun): the **International Health Center** in Galleria Strasburgo (also does dentistry, between Via Durini and Corso Europa, at #3, third floor, Metro: San Babila, tel. 02-7634-0720, www.ihc.it) and the **American International Medical Center** at Via Mercalli 11 (Metro: Missori or Crocetta, call for appointment, tel. 02-5831-9808, www.aimclinic.it).

Bookstores: The handiest major bookstore is **La Feltrinelli,** under the Galleria Vittorio Emanuele II (daily, tel. 02-8699-6903). The **American Bookstore** is at Via Manfredo Camperio 16, near Sforza Castle (closed Sun, Metro: Cairoli, tel. 02-878-920).

Laundry: Self-service laundry is hard to find in Milan; ask at your hotel for options. **Allwash,** at Via Savona 2, just off Via Zugna, is the closest launderette to the center. Take tram #14 (direction: Cim. Maggiore-Lorenteggio) to Piazzale Cantore, or go by Metro to Porta Genova and walk 5-10 minutes (daily 8:00-22:00, English instructions, tel. 800-030-653, www. allwash.it).

Soccer: For a dose of Europe's soccer mania (which many believe provides a necessary testosterone vent to keep Europe out of a third big war), catch a match while you're here. A.C. Milan and Inter Milan are the ferociously competitive home teams. Both teams play in the 85,000-seat **Meazza Stadium** (a.k.a. San Siro) most Sunday afternoons from September to June (ride Metro purple line 5 to San Siro Stadio, bring passport for security checks, www.acmilan.com or www.inter.it).

GETTING AROUND MILAN

By Public Transit: It's a pleasure to use Milan's great public transit system, called ATM ("ATM Point" info desk in Duomo Metro station, www.atm.it). The clean, spacious, fast, and easy **Metro** zips you nearly anywhere you may want to go, and trams and city buses fill in the gaps. The handiest Metro line for a quick visit is the yellow line 3, which connects Centrale station to the Duomo. The other lines are red (1), green (2), and purple (5). The Metro shuts down about half past midnight, but many trams continue until 1:00 or even 2:00. With 100 miles of track, Milan's classic, century-old yellow **trams** are both efficient and atmospheric.

A **single ticket,** valid for 90 minutes, can be used for one ride, including transfers, on all forms of transport (€1.50; sold at newsstands, tobacco shops, shops with *ATM* sticker in window, and at machines in subway stations). Other ticket options include a *carnet* (€13.80 for 10 rides—it's one magnetic ticket that can be validated 10 times, but only by a single user); a **24-hour pass** (€4.50, worth-

MILAN

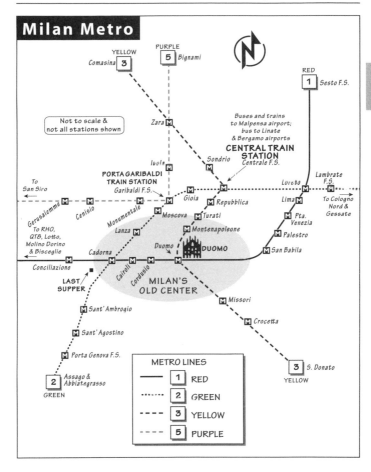

while if you take at least four rides); and a **48-hour pass** (€8.25, pays off with six rides). Tickets must be run through the machines at Metro turnstiles when you enter and leave the station. On trams, the machines are at the front and rear and you need only validate upon entry. You also need to validate if transferring.

By Taxi: Small groups go cheap and fast by **taxi** (drop charge-€3.30, €1.10/kilometer; €5.40 drop charge on Sun and holidays, €6.50 from 21:00 to 6:00 in the morning). It can be easier to walk to a taxi stand than to flag down a cab. Handy stands are at Piazza del Duomo and in front of Sforza Castle. Hotels and restaurants are also happy to call one for you (tel. 02-8585 or 02-6969). The free **MyTaxi** app (www.mytaxi.com), popular with younger and tech-savvy Milanese, lets you summon and pay for a taxi using your smartphone. After you enter your credit card number, the app charges you regular taxi fares and lets you add a tip. **Uber** Black

Milan at a Glance

▲▲▲**Duomo** Milan's showpiece cathedral, with an amazing ▲▲ roof you can walk on. **Hours:** Church—daily 8:00-19:00, last entry at 18:00; rooftop terraces—daily 9:00-19:00, last ascent at 18:00. See page 17.

▲▲**Galleria Vittorio Emanuele II** Glass-domed arcade on the main square, perfect for window shopping and people-watching anytime. See page 28.

▲▲**La Scala Opera House and Museum** The world's most prestigious opera house. **Hours:** Museum daily 9:00-17:30. See page 31.

▲▲**Basilica di Sant'Ambrogio** Historic, art-packed church dating to early Roman times. **Hours:** Mon-Sat 10:00-12:30 & 14:30-18:30, Sun 15:00-17:00. See page 37.

▲▲*The Last Supper* Leonardo da Vinci's masterpiece, displayed in the Church of Santa Maria delle Grazie (viewable only with a reservation). **Hours:** Tue-Sun 8:15-18:45 (last entry), closed Mon. See page 38.

▲▲**Brera Art Gallery** World-class collection of Italian paintings (13th-20th century), including Raphael, Caravaggio, Gentile da Fabriano, Piero della Francesca, Mantegna, and the Bellini brothers. **Hours:** Tue-Sun 8:30-19:15, closed Mon. See page 41.

▲▲**Sforza Castle** Milan's castle, whose highlight is an unfinished Michelangelo *pietà*. **Hours:** Museum—Tue-Sun 9:00-17:30, closed Mon; grounds—daily 7:00-19:00, until 18:00 Nov-March. See page 43.

▲**Duomo Museum** Church art and original sculptures from Milan's cathedral. **Hours:** Tue-Sun 10:00-18:00, closed Mon. See page 24.

▲**Piazza del Duomo** Milan's main square, full of energy, history, and pickpockets. See page 27.

▲**Museo del Novecento** Milan's 20th-century art collection, housed in the fascist-era City Hall. **Hours:** Mon 14:30-19:30; Tue-Wed, Fri, and Sun 9:30-19:30; Thu and Sat 9:30-22:30. See page 29.

▲**Piazza dei Mercanti** The evocative medieval heart of the city. See page 30.

▲**Gallerie d'Italia** Three adjacent palaces filled with 19th- and 20th-century Italian art. **Hours:** Tue-Sun 9:30-19:30, Thu until 22:30, closed Mon. See page 33.

▲**Pinacoteca Ambrosiana** Oldest museum in Milan, with works by Raphael, Leonardo, Botticelli, Titian, and Caravaggio. **Hours:** Tue-Sun 10:00-18:00, closed Mon. See page 34.

▲**Church of San Maurizio** The "Sistine Chapel of Lombardy," gorgeously frescoed by Bernardino Luini, a follower of Leonardo. **Hours:** Tue-Sun 9:30-19:30, closed Mon. See page 36.

▲**Leonardo da Vinci National Science and Technology Museum** Leonardo's designs illustrated in wooden models, plus a vast collection of historical and technological bric-a-brac and machines. **Hours:** Tue-Fri 10:00-18:00, Sat-Sun until 19:00, closed Mon. See page 38.

▲**Via Dante** Human traffic frolics to lilting accordions on one of Europe's longest pedestrian-only boulevards. See page 46.

▲**Naviglio Grande** Milan's old canal port—once a working-class zone, now an atmospheric nightspot for dinner or drinks. See page 46.

▲**Monumental Cemetery** Evocative final resting spot with tombs showcasing expressive art styles from 1870 to 1930. **Hours:** Tue-Sun 8:00-18:00, closed Mon. See page 47.

Risorgimento Museum Italy's rocky road to unification on one floor. **Hours:** Tue-Sun 9:00-13:00 & 14:00-17:30, closed Mon. See page 42.

Poldi Pezzoli Museum Italian paintings (15th-18th century), weaponry, and decorative arts **Hours:** Wed-Mon 10:00-18:00, closed Tue. See page 42.

Bagatti Valsecchi Museum 19th-century Italian Renaissance furnishings. **Hours:** Tue-Sun 13:00-17:45, closed Mon. See page 42.

Leonardo's Horse Gargantuan equestrian monument built from Leonardo's designs. See page 47.

MILAN

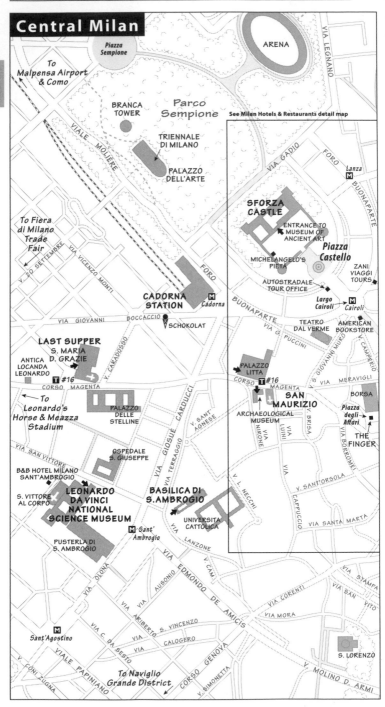

Central Milan

Piazza Sempione

ARENA

To Malpensa Airport & Como

BRANCA TOWER

Parco Sempione

See Milan Hotels & Restaurants detail map

TRIENNALE DI MILANO

PALAZZO DELL'ARTE

VIALE MOLIERE

To Fiera di Milano Trade Fair

V. 20 SETTEMBRE

VIA VICENZO MONTI

FORO

VIA GADIO

FORO

Lanza Ⓜ

VIA LEGNANO

BUONAPARTE

SFORZA CASTLE

ENTRANCE TO MUSEUM OF ANCIENT ART

MICHELANGELO'S PIETA

Piazza Castello

AUTOSTRADALE TOUR OFFICE

ZANI VIAGGI TOURS

CADORNA STATION

Ⓜ Cadorna

VIA GIOVANNI BOCCACCIO

SCHOKOLAT

LAST SUPPER

S. MARIA D. GRAZIE

ANTICA LOCANDA LEONARDO

Ⓣ #16

CORSO MAGENTA

VIA CARADOSSO

To Leonardo's Horse & Meazza Stadium

PALAZZO DELLE STELLINE

VIA GIOSUÈ CARDUCCI

VIA SANT'AGNESE

BUONAPARTE

VIA G. PUCCINI

TEATRO DAL VERME

Largo Cairoli

Ⓜ Cairoli

AMERICAN BOOKSTORE

VIA GIOVANNI MURO

VIA CAMPERIO

VIA MERAVIGLI

PALAZZO LITTA

Ⓣ #16

CORSO   MAGENTA

SAN MAURIZIO

ARCHAEOLOGICAL MUSEUM

VIA BRISA

VIA LUINI

VIA NIRONE

BORSA

Piazza degli Affari

THE FINGER

VIA BORROMEI

VIA SAN VITTORE

OSPEDALE S. GIUSEPPE

VIA TERRAGGIO

B&B HOTEL MILANO SANT'AMBROGIO

S. VITTORE AL CORPO

LEONARDO DA VINCI NATIONAL SCIENCE MUSEUM

PUSTERLA DI S. AMBROGIO

BASILICA DI S. AMBROGIO

Ⓜ Sant' Ambrogio

UNIVERSITA CATTOLICA

VIA LANZONE

V. L. NECCHI

V. SANT'ORSOLA

VIA CAPPUCCIO

VIA SANTA MARTA

Ⓜ Sant'Agostino

VIA OLONA

VIALE PAPINIANO

V. CONI ZUGNA

VIA C. DA SESTO

VIA ARIBERTO

AUSONIO

EDMONDO DE AMICIS

S. VINCENZO

VIA   CALOGERO

CORSO   GENOVA

V. CAM

V. SIMONETTA

To Naviglio Grande District

VIA CORENTI

VIA MORA

V. MOLINO D. ARMI

VIA STAMPA

VIA SAN VITO

S. LORENZO

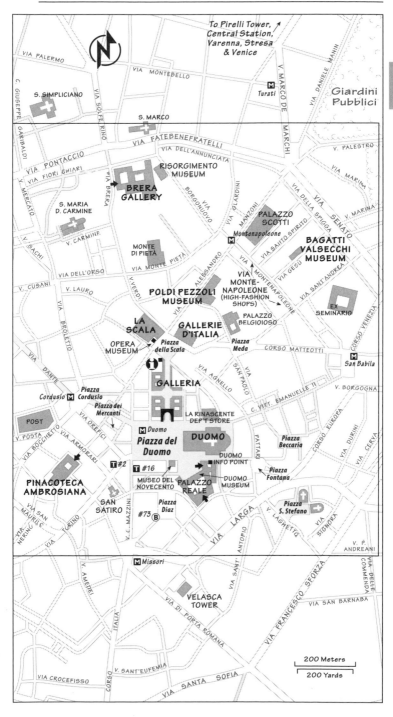

and UberLux operate in Milan and charge similar rates (but have faced legal challenges).

By Bike: Milan's public bike system, **BikeMi,** lets you set up a temporary subscription (€4.50/day, €9/week) online or at an "ATM Point" public transit info office (a handy one is in the Duomo Metro station). You'll receive a user code and password, allowing you to pick up a bike at any BikeMi station (generally located near Metro stations). Enter your code and password on the keypad, grab the assigned bike, and you're on your way (first 30 minutes free, then €0.50/30 minutes up to 2 hours, after that €2/hour, www. bikemi.com). Download the BikeMi app to see available bikes and parking spots.

Tours in Milan

🎧 To sightsee on your own, download my free Milan's Duomo Neighborhood audio tour.

Local Guides

Lorenza Scorti is a hardworking young guide who knows her city's history and how to teach it (€160/3 hours, €320/6 hours, same price for individuals or groups, evenings OK, mobile 347-735-1346, lorenza.scorti@libero.it). **Sara Cerri** is another good licensed local guide who enjoys passing on her knowledge (€195/3 hours, then €50/hour, mobile 380-433-3019, www.walkingtourmilan.it, walkingtourmilan@gmail.com). **Ludovic Charles Goudin** is energetic and has a passion for teaching art (€180/3 hours, mobile 331-289-3464, ludovicgoudin@icloud.com).

Walking and Bus Tours with *The Last Supper*

If your visit to Milan is fast approaching and you can't get a reservation for *The Last Supper,* consider joining a walking or bus tour that includes a guided visit to Leonardo's masterpiece. These €60-75 tours (usually three hours) also take you to top sights such as the Duomo, Galleria Vittorio Emanuele II, La Scala Opera House, and Sforza Castle. Ideally book at least a week in advance, but it's worth a try at the last minute, too.

For the best experience, I'd book a walking tour with **Veditalia** (www.veditalia.com) or **City Wonders** (www.citywonders.com). Both have good guides and solid reputations. The bus-and-walking tours are less satisfying, but you can try **Autostradale** ("Look Mi" tour, offices in passage at far end of Piazza del Duomo and in front of Sforza Castle, tel. 02-8058-1354, www.autostradaleviaggi.it) or **Zani Viaggi** (office disguised as a "tourist information" point, corner of Foro Buonaparte and Via Cusani at #18, near Sforza Castle, tel. 02-867-131, www.zaniviaggi.com).

Hop-On, Hop-Off Option: Zani Viaggi also operates

CitySightseeing Milano hop-on, hop-off buses (look for the red buses—easiest at Duomo and La Scala, €22/all day, €25/48 hours, buy on board, recorded commentary, www.milano.city-sightseeing. it). With a bus ticket, you can pay an additional €33 for a *Last Supper* reservation—exorbitant but worth considering for the wealthy and the desperate (April-Oct only).

Sights in Milan

Milan's core sights—the Duomo, Duomo Museum, and Galleria Vittorio Emanuele II—cluster within easy walking distance. ∩ Download my free Milan's Duomo Neighborhood audio tour, available in 2018, to link them in one convenient stroll. Also in the Duomo area are the Piazza della Scala and La Scala Opera House.

The city's other main sights—*The Last Supper,* Basilica di Sant'Ambrogio, Sforza Castle, and Brera Art Gallery—are scattered farther afield. It's easiest to reach them by public transportation.

▲▲▲DUOMO (CATHEDRAL)

The city's centerpiece is the third-largest church in Europe (after St. Peter's Basilica in Rome and Sevilla's cathedral). At 525 by 300 feet, the place is immense, with more than 2,000 statues inside (and another thousand outside) and 52 one-hundred-foot-tall, sequoia-size pillars representing the weeks of the year and the liturgical calendar. If you do two laps, you've done your daily walk. The church was built to hold 40,000 worshippers—the entire population of Milan when construction began.

A visit here has several elements. First, take in the overwhelming exterior from various angles, admiring its remarkable bulk and many spires and statues. Then go inside (requires a ticket) to see the church's vast nave, stained glass, historic tombs, and a quirky, one-of-a-kind statue of a flayed man. Nearby, a visit to the adjacent Duomo Museum lets you see the church's statues and details up close. Finally, take an elevator ride (or long stair climb) up to the Duomo rooftop for city views and a stroll through a forest of jagged church spires.

Cost: Duomo and Duomo Museum—€3, includes skippable

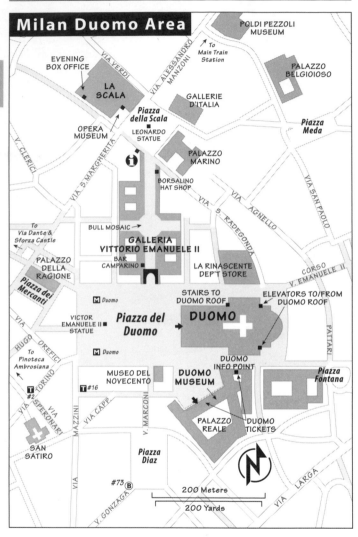

San Gottardo Church; rooftop terraces—€13 by elevator, €9 via stairs. To visit the archaeological area under the church, purchase the €7 ticket that includes the church and museum, or a combo-ticket that includes the rooftop terraces (€12-16); see website for details.

Hours: Duomo and archaeological area—daily 8:00-19:00, last entry at 18:00; Duomo Museum and San Gottardo Church—Tue-Sun 10:00-18:00, closed Mon, last entry at 17:00; rooftop terraces—daily 9:00-19:00, last ascent at 18:00.

Information: Church tel. 02-7202-2656, museum tel. 02-860-358, www.duomomilano.it.

Buying Tickets: Ticket booths are located on the south side of the cathedral: at the Duomo Museum (Tue-Sun 8:45-18:00, closed Mon), and just east of the museum (across from the Duomo's right transept) at #14a (daily 9:00-17:45, shorter hours Nov-April)—this location also hosts the **Duomo Info Point** office (daily 9:30-17:30). Ticket machines are available at both locations.

MILAN

Dress Code: Modest dress is required to visit the church. Don't wear shorts or anything sleeveless—even children.

Tours: A €6 audioguide for the church is available at a kiosk inside its main door (no rentals Sun, 1.5 hours).

⊙ Self-Guided Tour

Exterior

Stand facing the main facade. The Duomo is huge and angular, with prickly spires topped with statues. The style, Flamboyant Gothic, means "flame-like," and the church seems to flicker toward heaven with flames of stone. The facade is a pentagon, divided by six vertical buttresses, all done in pink-white marble. The dozens of statues, pinnacles, and pointed-arch windows on the facade are just a fraction of the many adornments on this architecturally rich structure.

For more than 2,000 years, this spot has been the spiritual heart of Milan—in 2014, archaeologists probing for ancient Roman ruins beneath the Duomo discovered the remains of what might be a temple to the goddess Minerva. A church has stood on this site since the days of the ancient Romans and St. Ambrose, but construction of the building we see today began in 1386. Back then, Europe was fragmented into countless tiny kingdoms and dukedoms, and the dukes of Milan wanted to impress their counterparts in Germany, France, and the Vatican with this massive cathedral. They chose the trendy Gothic style coming out of France, and stuck with it even after Renaissance-style domes came into vogue elsewhere in Italy. The cathedral was built not from ordinary stone, but from expensive marble, top to bottom. Pink Candoglia marble was rafted in from a quarry about 60 miles away, across Lake Maggiore and down a canal to a port at the cathedral—a journey that took about a week. Construction continued from 1386 to 1810, with final touches added as late as 1965.

The statues on the lower level of the facade—full of energy and movement—are early Baroque, from about 1600. Of the five doors, the center one is biggest. Made in 1907 in the Liberty Style (Italian Art Nouveau), it features the Joy and Sorrow of the Virgin Mary. Sad scenes are on the left, joyful ones on the right, and on

MILAN

top is the coronation of Mary in heaven by Jesus, with all the saints and angels looking on.

Topping the church (you may have to back up to see it) is its tallest spire. It rises up from the center of the Duomo to display a large golden statue of the Madonna of the Nativity, to whom the church is dedicated.

A Closer Look: Along the right side of the church are interesting views from every angle: the horizontal line of the long building, the verticals of the spires, and the diagonals of the flying buttresses supporting the roof. Get close to the facade's right corner to appreciate the many intricate details: a nude Atlas holding up the buttress, robed saints, relief panels of Bible scenes, and tiny faces—angry, smiling, happy, sad.

Stroll a little farther down the right to see the range of statues, from placid saints to thrashing nudes. These statues were made between the 14th and 20th centuries by sculptors from all over Europe. There are hundreds of them—each different. Midway up are the fanciful gargoyles (96 in total) that functioned as drain spouts. Look way up to see the statues on the tips of the spires...they seem so relaxed, like they're just hanging out, waiting for their big day.

The back end of the church (if you make it that far) is the oldest part, with the earliest stones, laid in the late 1300s. The sun-in-rose window was the proud symbol of the city's leading Visconti family. It's flanked by the angel telling Mary she's going to bear the Messiah. Nearby, find the shrine to the leading religion of the 21st century: soccer. The Football Team store is filled with colorful vestments and relics of local soccer saints.

Interior

• *Enter the church.*

Nave: It's the fourth-longest nave in Christendom, stretching more than 500 feet from the entrance to the stained-glass rose window at the far end. The apse at the far end was started in 1385. The wall behind you wasn't finished until 1520.  The style is Gothic, a rarity in Italy. Fifty-two tree-sized **pillars** rise to support a ribbed, pointed-arch ceiling, and the church is lit by glorious stained glass. At the far end, marking the altar, is a small tabernacle of a dome atop columns—a bit of an anomaly in a Gothic church (more on that later). Notice the little red light on the cross above the altar. This marks where a nail from the cross of Jesus is kept. This relic was brought to Milan by St. Helen (Emperor Constantine's moth-

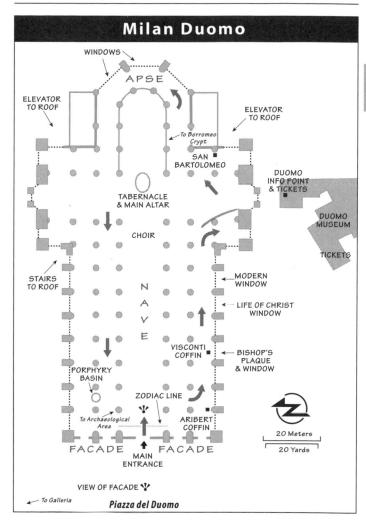

← To Galleria *Piazza del Duomo*

er) in the fourth century, when Milan was the capital of the western Roman Empire. It's on display for three days a year (in mid-Sept).

Closer to you, find the two single-stone marble pillars flanking the main door—the most precious ones in the church. Now, facing the altar, look high to the right, in the rear corner of the church, and find a tiny pinhole of white light. This is designed to shine a 10-inch sunbeam at noon onto the **bronze line** that runs across the floor, indicating where we are on the zodiac (but local guides claim they've never seen it work).

This 600-year-old church is filled with history. It represents the continuous line of bishops who have presided over Milan, stretching back to the days of St. Ambrose (c. 340-397). Let's see some of the earliest artifacts.

• *Wander deeper into the church, up the...*

Right Aisle: The first chapel along the right wall has the 1,000-year-old gray-stone coffin of **Aribert,** a bishop who predates the present building. Continuing along to the third chapel, you'll see a red coffin atop columns belonging to the noble **Visconti** family that commissioned this church.

The third bay also has a plaque where you can trace the uninterrupted rule of 144 local archbishops back to A.D. 51. Check out the **stained-glass window** above the plaque. Each window has 12 panels and 12 rows, creating 144 separate scenes. Find familiar scenes along the window's bottom level: Cain killing Abel, the Flood, and the drunkenness of Noah. The brilliant and expensive colored glass (stained, not painted) is from the 15th century. Bought by wealthy families seeking the Church's favor, the windows face south to get the most light. The altars below generally honor the patron who made each window possible. The windows' purpose was to teach the illiterate masses the way to salvation through stories from the Old Testament and the life of Jesus. On the opposite wall (left side), many of the windows are more modern—from the 16th to the 20th century—and are generally made of dimmer, cheaper painted glass. Many are replacements for ones destroyed by the concussion of WWII bombs that fell nearby.

The **fifth window** dates from 1470, "just" 85 years after the first stone of the cathedral was laid. The window shows the story of Jesus, from Annunciation to Crucifixion. In the bottom window, as the angel Gabriel tells Mary the news, the Holy Spirit (in the form of a dove) enters Mary's window and world. Compare the exquisite beauty of this window to the cruder 19th-century window on the right.

The **seventh window** is modern, from the 1980s. Bright and bold, it celebrates two local cardinals (whose tombs and bodies are behind glass). This memorial to Cardinal Ferrari and Cardinal Schuster, who heroically helped the Milanese out of their post-WWII blues, is a reminder that this great church is more than a tourist attraction—it's a living part of Milan.

• *Now take a few steps back into the nave for a view of the...*

Main Altar: The altar area is anchored by the domed tabernacle atop columns. This houses the receptacle that holds the Eucharist. Flanking the tabernacle are two silver statues of famous bishops. One is **St. Ambrose,** the influential fourth-century bishop who put Milan on the map and became the city's patron saint. The other is **St. Charles Borromeo,** the bishop who transformed the Duomo in the 16th century. Charles had inherited a cathedral that was barely half-finished. He re-energized the project, and commissioned the tabernacle.

While the rest of the church is Gothic, the altar is Baroque—a dramatic stage-like setting in the style of the Vatican in the 1570s. Borromeo was a great champion of the Catholic church, and this powerful style was a statement to counter the (mostly Gothic) Protestant churches of the north. Look up into the dome above the altar—a round dome on an octangular base, rising 215 feet. **Napoleon** crowned himself King of Italy under this dome in 1805. It was Napoleon who sped up construction, so that in 1810—finally—the church was essentially completed.

• *Before moving on, look to the rear, up at the ceiling, and see the fancy "carved"* **tracery** *on the ceiling's ribs. Nope, that's painted. It looks expensive, but paint is more affordable than carved stone. Now continue up the right aisle and into the south (right) transept. Find the bald statue.*

St. Bartolomeo Statue: This is a grotesque 16th-century statue of St. Bartolomeo, an apostle and first-century martyr skinned alive by the Romans. Examine the details (face, hands, feet) of the poor guy. He piously holds a Bible in one hand and wears his own skin like a robe. Carved by a student of Leonardo da Vinci, this is a study in human anatomy learned by dissection, forbidden by the Church at the time. Read the sculptor's Latin inscription on the base: "I was not made by Praxiteles"—the classical master of beautiful nudes—"but by Marco d'Agrate."

• *Walk toward the altar, checking out the fine 16th-century inlaid-marble* **floor.** *The black marble (quarried from Lake Como) is harder and more durable, while the lighter colors (white from Lake Maggiore, pink from Verona) look and feel more worn. At the altar, bear right around the corner 30 steps. You'll see a door marked* Scurolo di S. Carlo. *This leads down to the...*

Crypt of St. Charles Borromeo: Steps lead under the altar to the tomb of St. Charles Borromeo (1538-1584), the economic power behind the church. You can still see Charles' withered body inside the rock-crystal coffin. Charles was bishop of Milan, and the second most important hometown saint after St. Ambrose. Tarnished silver reliefs around the ceiling show scenes from Charles' life.

• *Now resurface and continue around the apse, looking up at the...*

Windows: The apse is lit by three huge windows, all 19th-century painted copies. The originals, destroyed in Napoleonic times, were made of precious stained glass.

• *From the apse, head back through the church toward the main entrance. Near the entrance stands a large* **basin** *of expensive purple porphyry. Made by Borromeo's favorite architect, Pellegrini, it was used to baptize infants. Now find the entrance and stairs that lead down to the...*

Archaeological Area: The church's "basement" is a maze of ruined brick foundations of earlier churches that stood here long before the present one. Milan has been an important center of Christianity since its beginning. In Roman times, Mediolanum's streets were 10 feet below today's level.

The highlight here is the scant remains of the eight-sided **Paleo-Christian Baptistery of San Giovanni.** It stands alongside the remains of a little church. Back then, since you couldn't enter the church until you were baptized (which didn't happen until age 18), churches had a little baptistery just outside for the unbaptized.

This humble baptistery may be one of the most significant places in all of Christianity. It was here that little St. Ambrose was baptized. Ambrose went on to become bishop here, and to mentor a randy and rebellious Roman named Augustine. On this spot in A.D. 387, Ambrose baptized the 31-year-old **Augustine of Hippo,** who later became one of Christianity's (and the world's) most influential thinkers, philosophers, and writers. And the rest—like this tour—is history.

More Duomo Sights

▲Duomo Museum (Museo del Duomo)

This museum, to the right of the Duomo in the Palazzo Reale, helps fill in the rest of the story of Milan's cathedral, and lets you see its original art and treasures up close (your Duomo ticket includes museum admission; see "Cost" and "Hours" in the Duomo listing, earlier). The collection lacks description (in any language) and is virtually meaningless without an audioguide (€5). It's worth a walk-through if you have an interest in old church art.

Visiting the Museum: Just after the ticket taker, notice (on the wall to your right) the original **inlaid-marble floor** of the Duomo. The black (from Lake Como) marble is harder. Go ahead, wear down the white a little more.

Now follow the one-way route. Among the early treasures of the cathedral is a 900-year-old, Byzantine-style **crucifix.** Made of copper gilded with real gold and nailed onto wood, it was part of the tomb of the archbishop of Milan. A copy is in today's cathedral.

You'll pass a big, wooden model of the church (we'll get a better look at this later, on the way out). Then you'll step through a long room with paintings, chalices, glass monstrances, and lifelike reliquary busts of Sts. Charles, Sebastian, and Thecla.

Look for the big statue of **St. George.** Although this is a copy, the 600-year-old original is among the cathedral's oldest statues and once stood on the front (and first constructed) spire of the Duomo. Some think this is the face of Duke Visconti—the man who started the cathedral. The museum is filled with statues and spires like this, carved of *marmo di Candoglia*—marble from Candoglia. The duke's family gave the entire Candoglia quarry (near Stresa) to the church for all the marble it would ever need.

You'll pop into a long room filled with more statues. On your left, gaze—as did pilgrims 500 years ago—into the eyes of **God the Father.** Made of wood, wrapped in copper, and gilded, this giant head covered the keystone connecting the tallest arches directly above the high altar of the Duomo.

Continue into a narrow room lined with grotesque **gargoyles.** When attached to the cathedral, they served two purposes: to scare away evil spirits and to spew rainwater away from the building.

Twist through several more rooms of statues big and small. In one long, brick-walled hall, watch on the left for **St. Paul the Hermit,** who got close to God by living in the desert. While wearing only a simple robe, he's filled with inner richness. The intent is for pilgrims to commune with him and feel at peace (but I couldn't stop thinking of the Cowardly Lion—"Put 'em up! Put 'em up!").

A few steps beyond Paul, look for the 15th-century dandy with the rolled-up contract in his hand. That's Visconti's descendant, Galeazzo Sforza, and if it weren't for him, the church facade might still be brick as bare as the walls of this room. The contract he holds makes it official—the church now owns the marble quarry (and it makes money on it to this day).

In the next room, study the brilliantly gilded and dynamic statue *God the Father* (1554). Also keep an eye out for a sumptuous Flanders-style **tapestry,** woven of silk, silver, and gold. Half a millennium ago, this hung from the high altar. In true Flemish style, it weaves vivid details of everyday life into the theology. It tells the story of the Crucifixion by showing three scenes at once. Note the exquisite detail, down to the tears on Mary's cheeks.

Next you'll step through a stunning room with 360 degrees of gorgeous **stained glass** from the 12th to 15th century, telling the easily recognizable stories of the Creation, the Tower of Babel, and David and Goliath. Take a close look at details that used to be too far above the cathedral floor to be seen clearly.

Farther on, you'll reach a display of **terra-cotta panels** juxtaposed with large **monochrome paintings** (1628) by Giovanni Battista Crespi. After Crespi finished the paintings, they were translated into terra-cotta, and finally sculpted in marble to decorate the doorways of the cathedral. Study Crespi's *Creation of Eve (Creazione di Eva)* and its terra-cotta twin. This served as the model for the marble statue that still stands above the center door on the church's west portal (1643). You'll pass a few more of these scenes, then hook into a room with the original, stone-carved, swirling *Dancing Angels,* which decorated the ceiling over the door.

• *When you reach the doors leading into the museum shop, make a U-turn to see the final exhibits.*

After passing several big tapestries, and a huge warehouse where statues are stacked on shelves stretching up to the ceiling, you'll reach the *Frame of the Madonnina* (1773). Standing like a Picasso is the original iron frame for the statue of the Virgin Mary that still crowns the cathedral's tallest spire. In 1967, a steel replacement was made for the 33 pieces of gilded copper bolted to the frame. The carved-wood face of Mary (in the corner) is the original mold for Mary's cathedral-crowning copper face.

Soon you'll get a better look at that **wooden model** of the Duomo. This is the actual model used in the 16th century by the architects and engineers to build the church. This version of the facade wasn't built, and other rejected facades line the walls.

On your way out, you'll pass models for the Duomo's doors. And stepping outside, as your eyes adjust to the sunlight, you'll see the grand church itself—looking so glorious thanks to the many centuries of hard work you've just learned about.

▲▲Duomo Rooftop

Strolling between the frilly spires of the cathedral rooftop terraces is the most memorable part of a Duomo visit. You can climb the

stairs or take the elevators (for specifics, see "Cost" and "Hours" in the Duomo listing, earlier). On the left side, the stairs are in front of the transept, and the elevator is behind it. (Even those taking the elevator will have to climb some stairs.) On the right side, look for the elevator behind the transept.

Once up there, you'll loop around the rooftop, wandering through a fancy forest of spires with great views of the city, the square, and—on clear days—the crisp and jagged Alps to the north. And, 330 feet above everything, La Madonnina overlooks it all. This 15-foot-tall gilded Virgin Mary is a symbol of the city.

As you emerge from the stairs or lift, you first walk along the **lower side-terrace.** You'll enjoy close-ups of fanciful gargoyles, statue-topped spires, and ever-changing views of the rows of flying buttresses (which, on this lavishly ornamented Gothic church, are more decorative than functional).

Next you climb a richly carved staircase to the sloping **rooftop**—directly above the nave. As you wander among the spires, pick any single one and appreciate its details. At the **spires'** base is the marble "fence" that surrounds the entire rooftop, with its pointed arches topped with pinnacles, which themselves are mostly crowned with crosses. Each spire is supported by blocks of Candoglia marble, with its pink-white-green-blue hues (which blend into gray).

On the next level up, the spires have vertical ribs and saints in cages. Continuing up, they get more ornate, with flamboyant flames that flicker upward toward still more saints posing beneath church-like awnings. Finally, the spire tapers into a slender point, topped with a lifelike **saint** who gazes out over the city. The church has 135 spires—all similar, yet each different. No wonder it took 600 years to carve it all.

At the **counter-facade** (the back side of the church's false-front facade), find a few 20th-century details that are among the last things done. To the left (as you face toward the Piazza del Duomo), find carved reliefs with boxing scenes. Just above and to the right of the boxing scenes is a relief of carved foliage. The proud-looking face peering out from the leaves is none other than the WWII dictator, Benito Mussolini.

Before leaving, check out the great **views** of the city. To the east, you can peer down into the Piazza del Duomo, 20 stories below.

To the south of the Duomo is the red-brick, octagonal, statue-topped bell tower of San Gottardo Church, built in the 1300s by the same Visconti family that began the Duomo. The hard-to-miss Velasca Tower (Torre Velasca) is a top-heavy skyscraper from the 1950s (modeled on medieval watchtowers such as those at the Sforza Castle), which became a symbol of Milan's rise from the ashes of World War II.

Looking north, there's a skyline of a dozen-plus skyscrapers. At the far right of the group is the 32-story Pirelli Tower, a slender rectangle with tapering sides, which proclaimed Italy's postwar "economic miracle." The UniCredit Tower (from 2011), with its 750-foot-high rocket-like spire, is Italy's tallest building, and represents Milan's future.

AROUND THE DUOMO

▲**Piazza del Duomo**

Stand in the center of Milan's main square and take in the scene. Before you rises the massive, prickly facade of Milan's cathedral, the Duomo. The huge equestrian **statue** in the center of the piazza is Victor Emmanuel II, the first king of Italy. He's looking at the grand **Galleria**

named for him. The words above the triumphal arch entrance read: "To Victor Emmanuel II, from the people of Milan."

To the right of the Duomo are the twin fascist buildings of the Arengario Palace. Mussolini made grandiose speeches from their balconies. Study the buildings' relief panels, which tell—with fascist melodrama—the history of Milan. Today the palace houses the **Museo del Novecento** (described later).

Directly to the right of the Duomo is the historic ducal palace, the Palazzo Reale, which now houses the **Duomo Museum** (described earlier). The palace was redone in the Neoclassical style by Empress Maria Theresa in the late 1700s, when Milan was ruled by the Austrian Habsburgs.

Behind the Victor Emmanuel II statue (opposite the cathedral, about a block beyond the square), hiding in a small courtyard, is **Piazza dei Mercanti,** the center of medieval Milan (described later).

And all around you in Piazza del Duomo is a classic European scene and a local gathering point. Professionals scurry, fashion-forward kids loiter, and young thieves peruse.

▲▲Galleria Vittorio Emanuele II

This breathtaking four-story glass-domed arcade, next to Piazza del Duomo, is a symbol of Milan. The iron-and-glass shopping mall (built during the age of Eiffel and the heady days of Italian unification) showcased a new, modern era. It was the first building in town to have electric lighting, and from its inception it's been an elegant and popular meeting place. (Sadly, its designer, Giuseppe Mengoni, died the day before the gallery opened.) Here you can turn an expensive cup of coffee into a good value by enjoying some of Europe's best people-watching.

The venerable **Bar Camparino** (at the Galleria's Piazza del Duomo entry), with a friendly staff and a period interior, is the former haunt of famous opera composer Giuseppe Verdi and conductor Arturo Toscanini, who used to stop by after their performances at La Scala. It's a fine place to enjoy a drink and people-watch (€3.70 for an espresso is a great deal to take a seat, relax and enjoy the view, or pay €1.10 at the bar just to experience the scene). The café is named after the Campari family (its first owners), originators of the famous red Campari bitter (Tue-Sun 7:30-20:00, closed Mon and Aug, tel. 02-8646-4435).

Wander around the Galleria. Its art celebrates the establishment of Italy as an independent country. Around the central dome, patriotic mosaics symbolize the four major continents (sorry, Australia). The mosaic floor is also patriotic. The white cross in the center is part of the king's coat of arms. The she-wolf with Romulus and Remus (on the south side—facing Rome) honors the city that, since 1870, has been the national capital. On the west side (facing Torino, the provisional capital of Italy from 1861 to 1865), you'll find that city's symbol: a *torino* (little bull). For good luck, locals step on his irresistible little

testicles. Two local girls explained to me that it works better if you spin—two times, and it must be clockwise. Find the poor little bull and observe for a few minutes...it's a cute scene. With so much spinning, the mosaic is replaced every few years.

Luxury shops have had outlets here from the beginning. Along with Gucci, Louis Vuitton, and Prada, you'll find Borsalino (at the end near Piazza della Scala), which has been selling hats here since the gallery opened in 1877.

If you cut through the Galleria to the other side, you'll pop out at Piazza della Scala, with its famous opera house and the Gallerie d'Italia (all described later).

▲Museo del Novecento

Milan's art of the 1900s *(Novecento)* fills the two buildings of the Arengario Palace, Mussolini's fascist-era City Hall. In the beautifully laid-out museum, you'll work your way up the escalators and through the last century, one decade at a time. Each section is well described, and the capper is a fine panoramic view over Piazza del Duomo through grand fascist-era arches. The museum makes it clear that Milan—a trendy city today—has been setting design trends since the start of the *Novecento*.

Cost and Hours: €5, free from two hours before closing and Tue after 14:00; Mon 14:30-19:30; Tue-Wed, Fri, and Sun 9:30-19:30; Thu and Sat 9:30-22:30; last entry one hour before closing, audioguide-€5, facing Piazza del Duomo at Via Marconi 1, tel. 02-8844-4072, www.museodelnovecento.org.

Visiting the Museum: As you spiral up the ramp, pause at the large painting, *The Fourth Estate,* to gaze into the eyes of proud workers getting off their shift. Painted in 1901, the work was a bold manifesto of a new era, and is a good introduction to the revolutionary spirit of the museum.

On the **second floor,** minor works by Picasso, Matisse, Mondrian and others are a snapshot of "Modern Art" trends around Europe as the 1900s began. Next you see how they inspired Italy's artists. Boccioni followed northern Europe's lead, evolving from a placid painter of realistic portraits to a bold sculptor of swirling forms. He captured a world in high-tech motion—i.e., "Futurism."

Escalate up to the **third floor** to see Giorgio de Chirico's brooding canvases of long shadows and empty architecture—Italy's great contribution to the movement called Surrealism.

The **fourth floor** focuses on the actual *Novecento* Italiano movement of the 1920s, which was based in Milan. These artists tried to merge Italy's classic roots (of monumental ancient Roman art and geometrically solid Renaissance art) with abstract styles and the revivalist spirit of the Mussolini years.

Continuing up to the **fifth floor,** you emerge into a glass-walled space (often hosting temporary installations) with great views over Piazza del Duomo. Find the stairs up to the top room, with canvases by Lucio Fontana. In the 1950s and '60s, Fontana made his mark by slicing and puncturing canvases to transform a two-dimensional "painting" into a three-dimensional "sculpture." Fontana also did the room's textured ceiling and a large neon sculpture elsewhere on floor 5.

▲Piazza dei Mercanti

This small square, the center of political power in 13th-century Milan, hides one block off Piazza del Duomo (directly opposite the cathedral). A strangely peaceful place today, it offers a fine smattering of historic architecture that escaped the bombs of World War II.

The arcaded, red-brick building that dominates the center of the square was the City Hall (Palazzo della Ragione); its arcades once housed the market hall. Overlook-

ing the wellhead in the middle of the square is a balcony with coats of arms—this is where new laws were announced. Eventually two big families—Visconti and Sforza—took power, Medici-style, in Milan; the snake is their symbol. Running the show in Renaissance times, these dynasties shaped much of the city we see today, including the Duomo and the fortress. In 1454, the Sforza family made peace with Venice while enjoying a friendship with the Medici in Florence (who taught them how to become successful bankers). This ushered in a time of stability and peace, when the region's major city-states were run by banking families, and money was freed up for the Renaissance generation to make art, not war.

This square also held the Palace of Justice (the 16th-century courthouse with the clock tower), the market (not food, but crafts: leather, gold, and iron goods), the bank, the city's first university, and its prison. All the elements of a great city were right here on the "Square of the Merchants."

ON PIAZZA DELLA SCALA

To reach these sights, cut through the Galleria Vittorio Emanuele II from Piazza del Duomo.

Piazza della Scala

This smart little traffic-free square, between the Galleria and the opera house, is dominated by a statue of Leonardo da Vinci. The statue (from 1870) is a reminder that Leonardo spent his best 20 years in Milan, where he found well-paid, steady work. He was the brainy darling of the Sforza family (who dominated Milan as the Medici family dominated Florence). Under the great Renaissance genius stand four of his greatest "Leonardeschi." (He apprenticed a sizable group of followers.) The reliefs show his various contributions as a painter, architect, and engineer. Leonardo, wearing his hydro-engineer hat, reengineered Milan's canal system, complete with locks. (Until the 1920s, Milan was one of Italy's major ports, with canals connecting the city to the Po River and Lake Maggiore.)

The statue of Leonardo is looking at a plain but famous Neoclassical building, arguably the world's most prestigious opera house (described next).

▲▲La Scala Opera House and Museum

Milan's famous Teatro alla Scala opened in 1778 with an opera by Antonio Salieri (Mozart's wannabe rival). Today, opera buffs

can get a glimpse of the theater and tour the adjacent museum's extensive collection, featuring Verdi's top hat, Rossini's eyeglasses, Toscanini's baton, Fettuccini's pesto, original scores, diorama stage sets, busts, portraits, and death masks of great composers and musicians. For true devotees, La Scala is the Mecca of the religion of opera.

Cost and Hours: €8, daily 9:00-17:30, Piazza della Scala, tel. 02-8879-7473, www.teatroallascala.org.

Visiting the Museum: The main reason to visit the museum is the opportunity (on most days) to peek into the actual theater. The stage is as big as the seating area on the ground floor. (You can see the towering stage box from Piazza della Scala across the street.) A recent renovation corrected acoustical problems caused by WWII bombing and subsequent reconstruction. The royal box is just below your vantage point, in the center rear. Take in the ornate red-velvet seats, white-and-gold trim, the huge stage and orchestra pit, and the massive chandelier made of Bohemian crystal.

The museum itself is a handful of small rooms with low-tech displays. Room 1 has antique musical instruments—some are familiar-looking keyboards and guitars, some are strange and weirdly shaped. Room 2 takes you to the roots of opera in *commedia dell'arte*—those humorous plays of outsized characters and elaborate costumes, like clever harlequins and buffoonish doctors in masks. Room 3 features Liszt's grand piano, still in playing condition.

Room 4's paintings lead you through opera's heyday in Milan. There's a street scene of La Scala in 1852, with fancy carriages and well-dressed ladies and gents. Find portraits of great opera composers like portly Rossini, sideburned Donizetti, and thick-bearded Verdi (flanked by his two wives). In the glass case are miniature portraits of famous opera composers and singers, as well as Napoleon's sword. Pass through Room 5 and into Room 6, with a glass case holding a snip of Mozart's hair and a cast of Chopin's slender hand. (The stairs lead up to temporary exhibits.)

Room 7 features many of opera's all-stars. In the glass case is a snip of Verdi's hair, scores by Verdi and Puccini, and batons of the great conductor (and music director of La Scala) Toscanini, who's practically a saint in this town. The room's portraits bring opera into the modern age. There's the great composer Puccini whose accessible operas seem to unfold like realistic plays that just happen to be sung. The great early-20th-century tenor Enrico Caruso brought sophisticated Italian opera to barbaric lands like America. There are portraits of renowned sopranos (and world-class divas) Maria Callas and Renata Tebaldi.

Performances in the Opera House

The show goes on at the world-famous La Scala Opera House, which also hosts ballet and classical concerts. There are performances every month except August, and showtime is usually at 20:00 (for information, check online or call Scala Infotel Service, daily 9:00-18:00, tel. 02-7200-3744). On the opening night of an opera, a dress code is enforced for men (suit and tie).

Advance Booking: Seats sell out quickly. Online tickets go on sale two months before performances (www.teatroallascala.org). You can also book through an automated phone system: Call 02-

MILAN

860-775 and press 2 for English. Tickets are also sold at an office beneath Piazza del Duomo (daily 12:00-18:00, use stairs down in front of the Duomo and follow *ATM Point* signs). The "evening box office" *(Biglietteria Serale)* at the opera house itself—see below—opens 2.5 hours before showtime.

Same-Day Tickets: On performance days, 140 sky-high, restricted-view, peanut-gallery tickets are offered at a low price (generally less than €15) at the box office (located down the left side of the theater toward the back on Via Filodrammatici, and marked with *Biglietteria Serale* sign). It's a bit complicated: Show up at 13:00 with an official ID (driver's license or passport) to put your name on a list (one ticket per person; for popular shows people start lining up long before, weekends tend to be busiest), then return at 17:00 for the roll call. You must be present when your name is called to receive a voucher, which you'll then show at the window to purchase your ticket. (Matinees and symphonic concerts follow a different timetable; check the website.) Finally, one hour before showtime, the box office sells any remaining tickets at a 25 percent discount.

▲Gallerie d'Italia

This museum fills three adjacent buildings on Piazza della Scala with the amazing art collections of a bank that once occupied part

of this space. The bank building's architecture is early-20th-century, Tiffany-like Historicism, with a hint of Art Nouveau; it's connected to two impressive palazzos that boast the nicest Neoclassical interiors I've seen in Milan. They are filled with exquisite work by 19th- and 20th-century Italian painters.

Cost and Hours: €5, more during special exhibits, includes audioguide, free first Sun of the month; open Tue-Sun 9:30-19:30, Thu until 22:30, closed Mon, last entry one hour before closing; across from La Scala Opera House at Piazza della Scala 6, toll-free tel. 800-167-619, www.gallerieditalia.com.

Visiting the Museum: Enter through the bank building facing Piazza della Scala and take the red-velvet stairs to the basement to pick up an audioguide (also downstairs is a bag check, WCs, and the original bank vault, which now stores racks and racks of paintings not on display).

Back upstairs, head into the main atrium of the bank, and consider the special exhibits displayed there. Then, to tackle the permanent art collection in chronological order, head to the far end of the complex and work your way back (follow signs for *Palazzo Anguissola Antona Traversi* and *Palazzo Brentani*). You'll go through

MILAN

the café back into the Neoclassical palaces, where you'll trace the one-way route through the "Da Canova a Boccioni" exhibit, including marble reliefs by the Neoclassical sculptor Antonio Canova and Romantic paintings by Francesco Hayez. Upstairs, you'll see dramatic and thrilling scenes from the unification of Italy, as well as beautiful landscapes and cityscapes, especially of Milan. (An entire room is devoted to depictions of the now-trendy Naviglio Grande canal area in its workaday prime.)

On your way back to the bank building and the rest of the exhibit, take a moment to poke around the courtyard to find the *officina di restituzioni alle gallerie*—a lab where you can watch art restorers at work. Rejoining the permanent exhibit, you'll see paintings from the late 19th and early 20th centuries: Romantic landscapes; hyperrealistic, time-travel scenes of folk life; and Impressionism. Finally, you'll catch up to the art of the late 20th century, tucked between old bank-teller windows.

WEST OF THE DUOMO
These sights are listed roughly in the order you'll reach them as you travel west from Piazza del Duomo. The first one is just a few short blocks from the cathedral, while the last is just over a mile away.

▲Pinacoteca Ambrosiana
This oldest museum in Milan was inaugurated in 1618 to house Cardinal Federico Borromeo's painting collection. It began as a teaching academy, which explains its many replicas of famous works of art. Highlights include original paintings by Botticelli, Caravaggio, and Titian—and, most important, a huge-scale sketch by Raphael (may be under restoration when you visit) and a rare oil painting by Leonardo da Vinci.

Cost and Hours: €15, Tue-Sun 10:00-18:00, closed Mon, last entry one hour before closing, audioguide-€3, near Piazza del Duomo at Piazza Pio XI 2, Metro: Duomo or Cordusio, tel. 02-806-921, www.ambrosiana.eu.

Visiting the Museum: Pick up the English-language map locating the rooms and major works I highlight below, and rent the audioguide (covers both permanent and special exhibits). Then head upstairs to begin your visit.

Raphael's Cartoon (Room 5): Filling an entire wall, this drawing served as an outline for Raphael's famous *School of Athens* fresco at the Vatican Museums. (A cartoon—*cartone* in Italian—is a full-size sketch that's used to transfer a design to another surface.) While the Vatican's much-adored fresco is attributed entirely to Raphael, it was painted mostly by his students. But this *cartone* was wholly sketched by the hand of Raphael. To transfer the fresco design to the wall, his assistants riddled this cartoon with pinpricks along the outlines of the figures, stuck it to the wall of the pope's study, and then applied a colored powder. When they removed the *cartone,* the figures' shapes were marked on the wall, and completing the fresco was a lot like filling in a coloring book. Also in this room, look for Caravaggio's naturalistic *Basket of Fruit.*

Jan Brueghel (Room 7): As Cardinal Borromeo was a friend of Jan Brueghel, this entire room is filled with delightful works by the artist and other Flemish masters. Study the wonderful detail in Brueghel's *Allegory of Fire* and *Allegory of Water.* The Flemish paintings are extremely detailed—many are painted on copper to heighten the effect—and offer an insight into the psyche of the age. If the cardinal were asked why he enjoyed paintings that celebrated the secular life, he'd likely say, "Secular themes are God's book of nature."

Leonardo Hall (Room 24): During his productive Milan years, Leonardo painted *Portrait of a Musician*—as delicate, mysterious, and thought-provoking as the *Mona Lisa.* (This is the only one of his canvases that remains in Milan.) The large fresco filling the far wall—with Christ receiving the crown of thorns—is by Bernardino Luini, one of Leonardo's disciples. But I find the big replica painting of *The Last Supper* most interesting. When the cardinal realized that Leonardo's marvelous frescoed original was fading, he commissioned Andrea Bianchi to create a careful copy to be displayed here for posterity. Today, this copy gives a rare chance to appreciate the original colorful richness of the now-faded masterpiece.

Piazza degli Affari and a Towering Middle Finger

This square and monument mark the center of Milan's financial district. The bold fascist buildings in the neighborhood were built in the 1930s under Mussolini. Italy's major stock exchange, the Borsa, faces the square. Stand in the center and appreciate the modern take on ancient aesthetics (you're standing atop the city's ancient Roman theater). Find the stern statues representing various labors and occupations and celebrating the nobility of workers— typical whistle-while-you-work fascist themes. Then notice the equally bold modern statue in the center. After a 2009 contest to find the most appropriate sculpture to grace the financial district, this was the winner. With Italy's continuing financial problems, here we see how "the 99 percent" feel when they stand before symbols of corporate power. (Notice how the finger is oriented—it's the 1 percent, and not the 99 percent, who's flipping the bird.) The 36-foot-tall, Carrara marble digit was made by Maurizio Cattelan, the most famous—or, at least, most controversial—Italian sculptor of our age. *L.O.V.E.,* as the statue is titled, was temporary at first. But locals liked it, and, by popular demand, it's now permanent.

▲Church of San Maurizio
(San Maurizio al Monastero Maggiore)

This church, part of a ninth-century convent built into a surviving bit of Milan's ancient Roman wall, dates from around 1500.

Despite its simple facade, it's a hit with art lovers for its amazing cycle of Bernardino Luini frescoes. Stepping into this church is like stepping into the Sistine Chapel of Lombardy.

Cost and Hours: Free, Tue-Sun 9:30-19:30, closed Mon, Corso Magenta 15 at the Monastero Maggiore, Metro: Cadorna or Cairoli, tel. 02-8645-0011.

Visiting the Church: Bernardino Luini (1480-1532), a follower of Leonardo, was also inspired by his contemporaries Michelangelo and Raphael. Sit in a pew and take in the art, which has the movement and force of Michelangelo and the grace and calm beauty of Leonardo.

Maurizio, the patron saint of this church, was a third-century Roman soldier who persecuted Christians, then converted, and eventually worked to stop those same persecutions. He's the guy standing on the pedestal in the upper right, wearing a bright yellow cape. The nobleman who paid for the art is to the left of the altar, kneeling and cloaked in black and white. His daughter, who joined the convent here and was treated as a queen (as nuns with noble connections were), is to the right. And all around are martyrs—identified by their palm fronds.

The adjacent **Hall of Nuns** (Aula delle Monache), a walled-off area behind the altar, is where cloistered sisters could worship apart from the general congregation. Fine Luini frescoes appear above and around the wooden crucifix. The Annunciation scene at the corners of the arch features a cute Baby Jesus zooming down from heaven (see Mary, on the right, ready to catch him). The organ dates from 1554, and the venue, with its fine acoustics, is popular for concerts with period instruments. Explore the pictorial Bible that lines the walls behind the wooden seats of the choir. Luini's landscapes were groundbreaking in the 16th century. Leonardo incorporated landscapes into his paintings, but Luini was among the first to make landscape the main subject of the painting.

Nearby: You'll exit the Hall of Nuns into the lobby of the adjacent **Archaeological Museum,** where you can pay €5 to see part of the ancient city wall and a third-century Roman tower.

▲▲Basilica di Sant'Ambrogio

One of Milan's top religious, artistic, and historic sights, this church was first built on top of an early Christian martyr's cemetery by St. Ambrose around A.D. 380, when Milan had become the capital of the fading (and Christian) western Roman Empire.

Cost and Hours: Free, Mon-Sat 10:00-12:30 & 14:30-18:30, Sun 15:00-17:00, Piazza Sant'Ambrogio 15, Metro: Sant'Ambrogio, tel. 02-8645-0895, www.basilicasantambrogio.it.

Visiting the Church: Ambrose was a local bishop and one of the great fathers of the early Church. Besides his writings, he's remembered for converting and baptizing St. Augustine of Hippo, who himself became another great Church father. The original fourth-century church was later (in the 12th century) rebuilt in the Romanesque style you see today.

As you step "inside" from the street, you emerge into an arcaded **atrium**—standard in many churches back when people weren't allowed to actually enter the church until they were baptized. The unbaptized waited here during Mass. The courtyard is textbook Romanesque, with playful capitals engraved with fanciful animals. Inset into the wall (right side, above the pagan sarcophagi) are stone markers of Christian tombs—a reminder that this church, like St. Peter's at the Vatican, is built upon an ancient Roman cemetery.

From the atrium, marvel at the elegant 12th-century **facade,** or west portal. It's typical Lombard medieval style. The local bishop would bless crowds from its upper loggia. As two different monastic communities shared the church and were divided in their theology, there were also two different bell towers.

Step into the **nave** and grab a pew. The mosaic in the apse features Jesus Pantocrator (creator of all) in the company of Milanese saints. Around you are pillars with Romanesque capitals and surviving fragments of the 12th-century frescoes that once covered the church.

The 12th-century **pulpit** sits atop a Christian sarcophagus dating from the year 400. Study its late-Roman and early-Christian iconography—on the side facing the altar, Apollo on his chariot morphs into Jesus on a chariot. You can see the moment when Jesus gave the Old Testament (the first five books, anyway) to his apostles.

The precious, ninth-century golden **altar** has four ancient porphyry columns under an elegant Romanesque 12th-century canopy. The entire ensemble was taken to the Vatican during World

War II to avoid destruction. That was smart—the apse took a direct hit in 1943. A 13th-century mosaic was destroyed; today we see a reconstruction.

Step into the **crypt,** under the altar, to see the skeletal bodies of three people: Ambrose (in the middle, highest) and two earlier Christian martyrs whose tombs he visited before building the church.

Nearby: For a little bonus after visiting the church, consider this: The **Benedictine monastery** next to the church is now Cattolica University. With its stately colonnaded courtyards designed by Renaissance architect Donato Bramante, it's a nice place to study. It's fun to poke around and imagine being a student here.

▲Leonardo da Vinci National Science and Technology Museum (Museo Nazionale della Scienza e Tecnica "Leonardo da Vinci")

The spirit of Leonardo lives here. Most tourists focus on the hall of Leonardo—the core of the museum—where wooden models illustrate his designs. But the rest of this immense collection of industrial cleverness is fascinating in its own right. There are exhibits on space exploration, mining, and radio and television (with some original Marconi radios); old musical instruments, computers, and telephones; chunks of the first transatlantic cable; and interactive science workshops. Out back are several more buildings containing antique locomotives and a 150-foot-long submarine from 1957. Ask for an English museum map from the ticket desk—you'll need it. On weekends, this museum is very popular with families, so come early or be prepared to wait in line.

Cost and Hours: €10, Tue-Fri 10:00-18:00, Sat-Sun until 19:00, shorter hours off-season, closed Mon year-round, Via San Vittore 21, Metro: Sant'Ambrogio; tel. 02-485-551, www.museoscienza.org.

▲▲Leonardo da Vinci's *The Last Supper* (L'Ultima Cena/Cenacolo Vinciano)

Decorating the former dining hall *(cenacolo)* of the Church of Santa Maria delle Grazie, this remarkable, exactingly crafted fresco by Leonardo da Vinci is one of the ultimate masterpieces of the Renaissance. Reservations are mandatory and should be booked three months in advance (see options below).

Cost: €12, includes €2 reservation fee (9:30 and 15:30 visits cost €3.50 extra and include English tour). Free first Sun of the month (no reservations possible, show up by 8:00 to get a reserved time for later that day).

Hours: Open Tue-Sun 8:15-18:45 (last entry), closed Mon. Show up 20 minutes before your scheduled entry time. When an attendant calls your time, get up and move into the next room.

MILAN

Reservations: Mandatory timed-entry reservations can be made either online or by phone (through an outfit called Vivaticket). Reservations for each calendar month go on sale about three months ahead; for example, bookings for July open in early April. Spots are snapped up quickly, so plan ahead.

To book **online,** go to www.vivaticket.it, then enter "Cenacolo Vinciano" into the search bar at the top of the page. A calendar will show available time slots for the coming months.

If you book by **phone,** you'll have a greater selection of days and time slots to choose from, since the website doesn't reflect cancellations. Note that you can't reserve same-day tickets (tel. 02-9280-0360, from the US dial 011-39-02-9280-0360, office open Mon-Sat 8:00-18:30, closed Sun; the number is often busy—once you get through, select 2 for an English-speaking operator).

Tour Option: If you can't get a reservation, you can book a more expensive (€60-75) walking or bus tour that includes a guided visit to *The Last Supper*. These should be reserved at least one week ahead (for details, see "Tours in Milan," earlier).

Last-Minute Tickets: A few scattered same-day spots may be available due to cancellations. It's a low-percentage play, but you can try just showing up and asking at the desk—even if the *sold out* sign is posted (ideally when the office opens at 8:00, more likely on weekdays).

Audioguide: Consider the fine €3.50 audioguide. Its spiel fills every second of the time you're in the room—so try to start listening just before you enter (ideally in the waiting room while studying the reproduction of *The Last Supper*).

Getting There: The Church of Santa Maria della Grazie is a 10-minute walk from either Metro: Cadorna or Conciliazione. Or take tram #16 from the Duomo (direction: San Siro or Piazzale Segesta), which drops you off in front of the church.

Background: Milan's leading family, the Sforzas, hired Leonardo to decorate the dining hall of the Dominican monastery that adjoins the church (the Dominican order traditionally placed a Last Supper on one end of their refectories, and a Crucifixion at the other). Leonardo worked on the project from about 1492 until 1498. This gift was essentially a bribe to the monks so that the Sforzas could place their family tomb in the church. Ultimately, the French drove the Sforzas out of Milan, they were never buried here, and the Dominicans got a great fresco for nothing.

Deterioration began within six years of *The Last Supper*'s completion because Leonardo painted on the wall in layers, as he would on a canvas, instead of applying pigment to wet plaster in the usual fresco technique. The church was bombed in World War II, but—miraculously, it seems—the wall holding *The Last Supper* remained standing. A 21-year restoration project (completed in 1999) peeled away 500 years of touch-ups, leaving Leonardo's masterpiece faint but vibrant.

Visiting *The Last Supper:* To minimize damage from humidity, only 30 tourists are allowed in, every 15 minutes for exactly 15 minutes. While you wait, read the history of the masterpiece. As your appointed time nears, you'll be herded between several rooms to dehumidify, while doors close behind you and open up slowly in front of you.

And then the last door opens, you take a step, you look right, and...there it is. In a big, vacant, whitewashed room, you'll see faded pastels and not a crisp edge. The feet under the table look like negatives. But the composition is dreamy—Leonardo captures the psychological drama as the Lord says, "One of you will betray me," and the apostles huddle in stressed-out groups of three, wondering, "Lord, is it I?" Some are scandalized. Others want more information. Simon (on the far right) gestures as if to ask a question that has no answer. In this agitated atmosphere, only Judas (fourth from left and the only one with his face in shadow)—clutching his 30 pieces of silver and looking pretty guilty—is not shocked.

The circle meant life and harmony to Leonardo. Deep into a study of how life emanates in circles—like ripples on a pool hit by a pebble—Leonardo positioned the 13 characters in a semicircle. Jesus is in the center, from whence the spiritual force of God emanates, or ripples out.

The room depicted in the painting seems like an architectural extension of the church. The disciples form an apse, with Jesus as the altar—in keeping with the Eucharist. Jesus anticipates his sacrifice, his face sad, all-knowing, and accepting. His feet even foreshadow his death by crucifixion. Had the door, which was cut out in 1652, not been added, you'd see how Leonardo placed Jesus' feet atop each other, ready for the nail.

The perspective is mathematically correct, with Jesus' head

as the vanishing point where the converging sight lines meet. In fact, restorers found a tiny nail hole in Jesus' left eye, which anchored the strings Leonardo used to establish these lines. The table is cheated out to show the meal. Notice the exquisite lighting. The walls are lined with tapestries (as they would have been), and the one on the right is brighter in order to fit the actual lighting in the refectory (which has windows on the left). With the extremely natural effect of the light and the drama of the faces, Leonardo created a masterpiece.

NORTH OF THE DUOMO
▲▲Brera Art Gallery (Pinacoteca di Brera)

Milan's top collection of Italian paintings (13th-20th century) is world class, but it can't top those in Rome or Florence. Established in 1809 to house Napoleon's looted art, it fills the first floor above a prestigious art college. You'll dodge scruffy starving artists...and wonder if there's a 21st-century Leonardo in your midst.

Cost and Hours: €10, free first Sun of month, open Tue-Sun 8:30-19:15, closed Mon, last entry 45 minutes before closing, audioguide-€5 (useful, ID required, but museum has excellent English descriptions), free lockers, Via Brera 28, Metro: Lanza or Montenapoleone, tel. 02-722-631, www.pinacotecabrera.org.

Visiting the Museum: Enter the grand courtyard of a former monastery, where you'll be greeted by the nude *Napoleon with Tinkerbell* (by Antonio Canova). Climb the stairway (following signs to *Pinacoteca*), buy your ticket, and pick up an English map of the museum's masterpieces, some of which I've highlighted below. You'll follow a clockwise, chronological route through the huge collection.

In **Rooms IV-VI,** examine the altar paintings by late-Gothic master Gentile da Fabriano, hinting at the realism of the coming Renaissance (check out the lifelike flowers and realistic, bright gold paint—he used real gold powder). In the darkened section in the middle of **Room VII,** don't miss Andrea Mantegna's tour-de-force, *The Dead Christ.* It's a textbook example of feet-first foreshortening.

Next, to experience the peak of 16th-century Venetian painting, check out the color-rich canvases by the great masters Tintoretto and Veronese in **Room IX.**

Stop by the glass-enclosed restoration lab in **Room XVIII** to watch various conservation projects in progress.

In **Rooms XXII-XXIX,** you can see how Carlo Crivelli, a contemporary of Leonardo, employed Renaissance technique while clinging to the mystique of the Gothic Age (that's why I like him so much). In the next few rooms, don't miss Raphael's *Wedding of the Madonna* (Room XXIV), Piero della Francesca's *Madonna and Child with Saints* (also Room XXIV), and the gritty-yet-intimate realism of Caravaggio's *Supper at Emmaus* (Room XXIX).

Next, in **Rooms XXXI-XXXV,** you'll see Dutch and Flemish masters, including a big Rubens (Room XXXI). Room XXXV displays several of Canaletto's picture-postcards of Venetian cityscapes.

Finally, in **Room XXXVII,** you'll greet the modern age with Giuseppe Pellizza da Volpedo's rousing *Human Flood,* a study for his famous *Fourth Estate* (exhibited at the Museo del Novocento). Also in this room, spice things up with Francesco Hayez's hot and heavy *The Kiss (Il Bacio).*

Risorgimento Museum

With a quick 30-minute swing through this quiet one-floor museum, you'll get an idea of the interesting story of Italy's rocky road to unity: from Napoleon (1796) to the victory in Rome (1870). You'll see paintings, uniforms, monuments, a city model, and other artifacts. But limited English makes this best left to people already familiar with this important period of Italian history.

Cost and Hours: €5, free entry after 16:30 (Tue after 14:00), open Tue-Sun 9:00-13:00 & 14:00-17:30, closed Mon, just around the block from Brera Art Gallery at Via Borgonuovo 23, Metro: Montenapoleone, tel. 02-8846-4176, www.museodelrisorgimento.mi.it.

Poldi Pezzoli Museum

This classy house of art features Italian paintings of the 15th through 18th century, old weaponry, and lots of interesting decorative arts, such as a roomful of old sundials and compasses. It's all on view in a sumptuous 19th-century residence.

Cost and Hours: €10, Wed-Mon 10:00-18:00, closed Tue, audioguide-€1, Via Manzoni 12, Metro: Montenapoleone, tel. 02-794-889, www.museopoldipezzoli.it.

Bagatti Valsecchi Museum

This unique 19th-century collection of Italian Renaissance furnishings was assembled by two aristocratic brothers who spent a wad turning their home into a Renaissance mansion.

Cost and Hours: €9 includes audioguide, €6 on Wed; open Tue-Sun 13:00-17:45, closed Mon; Via Gesù 5, Metro: Montenapoleone, tel. 02-7600-6132, www.museobagattivalsecchi.org.

SFORZA CASTLE AND NEARBY
▲▲Sforza Castle (Castello Sforzesco)

The castle of Milan tells the story of the city in brick. Today it features a vast courtyard, a sprawling museum (with a few worthwhile highlights and Leonardo da Vinci connections), and—most importantly—a chance to see Michelangelo's final, unfinished *Pietà*.

Cost and Hours: €5, free entry after 16:30 (Tue after 14:00) and first Sun of the month; museum open Tue-Sun 9:00-17:30, closed Mon; castle grounds open daily 7:00-19:00, until 18:00 Nov-March; WCs and free/mandatory lockers downstairs from ticket counter, Metro: Cairoli or Lanza, tel. 02-8846-3700, www.milanocastello.it.

Background: Built in the late 1300s as a military fortress, Sforza Castle guarded the gate to the city wall and defended Milan from enemies "within and without." It was beefed up by the Sforza duke in 1450 in anticipation of a Venetian attack. Later, the Sforza family made it their residence, building their Renaissance palace into the fortress. It was even home to their in-house genius, Leonardo. (When he applied for a position with the Sforza family, he did so as a military engineer and contributed to the design of the ramparts.) During the time of foreign rule (16th-19th century), it was a barracks for occupying Spanish, French, and Austrian soldiers. Today it houses an array of museums, but I'd concentrate on the Michelangelo *Pietà* and the Museum of Ancient Art.

❍ Self-Guided Tour: This tour begins outside the fortress, then focuses on the highlights inside.

The Fortress: The **gate** facing the city center stands above a ditch that was once filled with water. A relief celebrates Umberto I, the second king of Italy. Above that, a statue of St. Ambrose, the patron of Milan (and a local bishop in the fourth century), oversees the action. Notice the diagram facing the gate that shows how the city was encircled first by a crude medieval wall, and then by a state-of-the-art 16th-century wall—of which this castle was a key element. It's apparent from the enormity of these walls that Milan was a strategic prize. Today, the walls are gone, giving the city two circular boulevards.

This immense brick fortress—exhausting at first sight—can only be described as heavy. Its three huge courtyards originally functioned as military parade grounds, but today host concerts and welcome the public. (The holes in the walls were for scaffolding.)

• *As you enter the main courtyard, look to your left to see the restored hospital building that houses the...*

Museo *Pietà* Rondanini (Michelangelo): This is a rare opportunity to enjoy a Michelangelo statue with relatively few crowds. Michelangelo died while still working on this piece, his fourth pietà—a representation of a dead Christ with a sorrowful Virgin Mary. While unfinished and seemingly a mishmash of corrections and reworks, it's a thought-provoking work by a genius at nearly 90 years old, who knows he's fast approaching the end of his life. The symbolism is of life and of death: Jesus returning to his mother, as two bodies seem to become one.

Michelangelo's more famous *pietà* at the Vatican (carved when he was in his 20s) features a beautiful, young, and astonished Mary. Here, Mary is older and wiser. Perhaps Mary is now better able to accept death as part of life...as is Michelangelo. The *pietà* at the Vatican is simple and clear, showing two different people: the mother holding her dead son. Contemplating the *Pietà Rondanini*, you wonder who's supporting whom. It's confused and complex, each figure seeming to both need and support the other.

This unfinished statue shows the genius of Michelangelo midway through a major rework—Christ's head is cut out of Mary's right shoulder, and an earlier arm is still just hanging there. Above Mary's right ear, you can see the remains of a previous face (eye, brow, and hairline).

And there's a certain power to this rawness. Walk around the back to see the strain in Mary's back (and Michelangelo's rough chisel work) as she struggles to support her son. The sculpture's elongated form hints at the Mannerist style that would follow.

Facing the *Pietà* is a bronze, life-size head, based on a death mask made at the artist's passing in 1564. Imagine him working on his *Pietà*—still vibrant and seeking.

• *From the* Pietà, *go over the little drawbridge in the back wall—directly across from where you entered the complex. Here you'll find the entrance to the...*

Museum of Ancient Art (Museo d'Arte Antica): This sprawling collection fills the old Sforza family palace with interesting medieval armor, furniture, early Lombard art, and much more.

In the first room, among ancient sarcophagi (with early-Christian themes), stands a fine 14th-century **equestrian statue**—a memorial to Bernabò Visconti. Of the four virtues, he selected only two (strength and justice) to stand beside his anatomically correct horse, opting out of love and patience.

Farther along, the room of **tapestries** is dominated by a big embroidery of St. Ambrose defeating the heretical Arians. While that was a fourth-century struggle, 12 centuries later, he was summoned back in spirit to deal with Protestants, in the form of Archbishop Borromeo. As a Counter-Reformation leader, with St. Peter's Basilica behind him, Ambrose stands tall and strong in defense of the Roman Church. The room is lined with 16th-century Flemish tapestries, which were easy to pack up quickly as the nobility traveled. These were typical of those used to warm chilly stone palaces.

Next, you'll come to the **Sala delle Asse** (may be closed for restoration when you visit). The Visconti family grew rich making silk in the Lake Como area. While plastered over for centuries, this room was restored around 1900. Not much sparkle survives, but you can appreciate the intricate canopy woven with branches and rope in complicated knots—the work of Leonardo himself, in 1498. The tiny Leonardo-esque painting of Madonna and Child is by Francesco Napoletano, a pupil of Leonardo. The painting's structure, anatomy, and subtle modeling of the color with no harsh lines *(sfumato)* are all characteristic of Leonardo. In the upper right, notice the castle, as it looked in 1495.

From here, you'll pass through rooms filled with weapons and armor from the 16th and 17th centuries.

• *At this point, you're free to go. But if you have a larger-than-average attention span, follow signs upstairs to the Decorative Arts Museum, then the Painting Gallery (Pinacoteca), and finally the Musical Instruments Museum. When you're done, consider popping out the back door of the fortress and taking a break in the lush Sempione Park (described next).*

Parco Sempione

This is Milan's equivalent of Central Park. With its circa-1900 English-style gardens, free Liberty-Style aquarium, views of the triumphal arch, and sprawling family-friendly grounds, this park is particularly popular on weekends.

A five-minute walk through the park, on the left, is the erector-set **Branca Tower** (Torre Branca), built for an exposition in the 1930s. For an inexpensive, commanding city view, you can ride an elevator as high as the Mary that crowns the Duomo (best in daylight, erratic hours—call or confirm at TI before making a special trip, Metro: Cadorna, www.museobranca.it, tel. 02-331-4120).

Next to the tower is the excellent **Triennale di Milano,** a design museum with changing exhibits that celebrate one of this city's fortes (www.triennale.org).

At the far end of the park is the monumental **Arco della Pace.** Originally an arch of triumph, it comes with Nike, goddess of victory, commanding a six-horse chariot. It was built facing Paris to welcome Napoleon's rule and to celebrate the ideals of the French Revolution, destined to lift Italy into the modern age. When the locals learned Napoleon was just another megalomaniac, they turned the horses around, their tails facing France.

▲Via Dante

This grand pedestrian boulevard and popular shopping street leads from Sforza Castle toward the town center and the Duomo. Via Dante was carved out of a medieval tangle of streets to celebrate Italian unification (c. 1870) and make Milan a worthy metropolis. Consequently, all the facades lining it are relatively new. Enjoy strolling this beautiful people zone, where you'll hear the whir of bikes and the lilting melodies of accordion players instead of traffic noise. Photo exhibits are frequently displayed up and down the street. In front of Sforza Castle, a commanding statue of Giuseppe Garibaldi, a hero of the unification movement, looks down one of Europe's longest pedestrian zones. From here you can walk to the Duomo and beyond (about 1.5 miles), appreciating Italian design both in shop windows and on smartly clothed Milanese.

AWAY FROM THE CENTER
▲Naviglio Grande (Canal District)

Milan, although far from any major lake or river, has a sizable port, literally called the "Big Canal." Since 1170, boats have been able to sail from Milan to the Mediterranean via the Ticino River (which flows into the Po River on its way to the Adriatic Sea).

Five hundred years ago, Leonardo helped design a modern lock system. During the booming Industrial Age in the 19th century—and especially with the flurry of construction after Italian unification—ships used the canals to bring in the marble and stone needed to make Milan the great city it is today. In fact, one canal (filled in during the 1930s) let barges unload stone right at the building site of the great cathedral. In the 1950s, landlocked Milan was the seventh-biggest port in Italy, as its canals aided in rebuilding the bombed-out city. Today, disused train tracks parallel the canal, old warehouse buildings recall the area's working-class heritage, and former workers' tenements—once squalid and undesirable—are being renovated. The once-rough area now dubbed Milan's "Little Venice" is trendy, traffic-free, and thriving with inviting bars and eateries. Come here for dinner or a late-afternoon drink (for recommendations, see "Eating in Milan," later).

Getting There: Ride the Metro (or tram #2) to Porta Genova, exit following signs to Via Casale, and walk the length of Via Casale one block directly to the canal. Most bars and restaurants are to the left, on both sides of the canal.

▲Monumental Cemetery (Il Cimitero Monumentale)

Europe's most artistic and dreamy cemetery experience, this grand place was built just after unification to provide a suitable final rest-

ing spot for the city's "famous and well-deserving men." Any cemetery can be evocative, but this one—with its super-emotional portrayals of the deceased and their heavenly escorts (in art styles c. 1870-1930)—is in a class by itself. It's a vast garden art gallery of proud busts and grim reapers, heartbroken angels and weeping widows, too-young soldiers and countless old smiles, frozen on yellowed black-and-white photos.

Cost and Hours: Free, Tue-Sun 8:00-18:00, closed Mon, pick up map at the entrance gate, ride Metro purple line 5 to Monumentale, tel. 02-8846-5600.

Leonardo's Horse

The largest equestrian monument in the world is a modern reconstruction of a model created in 1482 by Leonardo da Vinci for the

Sforza family. The clay prototype was destroyed in 1499 by invading French forces, who used it for target practice. In 1982, American Renaissance-art collector Charles Dent decided to build the 15-ton, 24-foot-long statue from Leonardo's design, planning to present it to the Italians in homage to Leonardo's genius. Unfortunately, Dent died be-

fore the project could be completed. In 1997, American sculptor Nina Akamu created a new clay model that became the template for the final statue; it was unveiled in 1999.

Getting There: The statue (free to view) is at a horse racetrack

on the western outskirts of town—ride Metro purple line 5 to San Siro Ippodromo.

Shopping in Milan

HIGH FASHION IN THE QUADRILATERAL

For world-class window shopping, visit the Quadrilateral, an elegant high-fashion shopping area around Via Montenapoleone, northeast of La Scala Opera House. This was the original Beverly Hills of Milan. In the 1920s, the top fashion shops moved in, and today it remains *the* place for designer labels. Most shops close Sunday and for much of August. On Mondays, stores open only after 16:00. In this land where fur is still prized, the people-watching is as entertaining as the window shopping. Notice also the exclusive penthouse apartments with roof gardens high above the scene. Via Montenapoleone and the pedestrianized Via della Spiga are the best streets.

Whether you're gawking or shopping, here's the best route: From Piazza della Scala, walk up Via Alessandro Manzoni to the Metro stop at Montenapoleone, browse down Via Montenapoleone, and cut left on Via Santo Spirito (lined with grand aristocratic palazzos—peek into the courtyard at #7). Across the street, step into the elegant courtyard at #10 to check out the café sitters and their poodles. Continue to the end of Via Santo Spirito, then turn right to window shop down traffic free Via della Spiga. After a few short blocks, turn right on Via Sant'Andrea and then left, back onto Montenapoleone, which leads you through a final gauntlet of temptations to Corso Giacomo Matteotti, near the Piazza San Babila. Then (for less-expensive shopping thrills), walk back to the Duomo down the pedestrian-only Corso Vittorio Emanuele II.

NEAR THE DUOMO

For a (slightly) more reasonably priced shopping excursion, step into **La Rinascente**—one of Europe's classic department stores. (It's around the left side as you face the front of the Duomo.) Simply riding the escalator up and up gives a fun overview of Italian design and marketing. The seventh floor is a top-end food circus with recommended restaurants, terrace views of the Duomo, and a public WC. The store's name translates roughly as "the place reborn" and fits its history. In an earlier life, this was a fine Art Nouveau-style building—until it burned down in 1918. Rebuilt, it was bombed in World War II and rebuilt once again (Mon-Thu 9:30-22:00, Fri-Sun until 23:00, has a VAT refund office, faces north side of the Duomo on Piazza del Duomo).

Heading away from the Duomo, stroll between the arcades

on the Corso Vittorio Emanuele II, surrounded by clothing stores and other tempting material pleasures. At Via Passarella, detour to the right to check out **Excelsior,** a bold high-end concept store. Moving walkways take you from level to colorful level with pulsing music and electronic art installations. If you're looking for the perfect €1,000 shirt, you've come to the right place. Otherwise, hit **Eat's Food Market,** a stylish deli in the basement, and pick up a tasty high-design salad to go (daily 9:00-22:00, Galleria del Corso 4, two long blocks behind the Duomo, tel. 027-630-7301).

Double back to the Corso Vittorio Emanuele II to continue shopping all the way to the San Babila Metro station (and the ritzy Quadrilateral area described earlier).

Nightlife in Milan

For evening action, check out the artsy Brera area in the old center, with several swanky sidewalk cafés to choose from and lots of bars that stay open late. Home to the local art university, this district has a sophisticated, lively people-watching scene. Another great neighborhood for nightlife, especially for a younger scene, is Naviglio Grande (the canal district), Milan's formerly bohemian, now-gentrified "Little Venice" (Metro: Porta Genova; tram #2).

There are always concerts and live music in the city at various clubs and concert halls. Specifics change quickly, so it's best to rely on the entertainment information in periodicals from the TI.

Sleeping in Milan

My recommended hotels are all within a few minutes' walk of a Metro station. With Milan's fine subway system, you can get anywhere in town in a flash.

Hotel prices in Milan rise and fall with the convention schedule. In March, April, September, and October, the city can be completely jammed by conventions, and hotel prices go sky-high; it's best to avoid the city entirely at these times if you can (for the convention schedule, see www.fieramilano.it). My rankings are based on regular prices, not the much-higher convention rates.

Summer is usually wide-open, with soft or discounted prices, though many hotels close in August for vacation. Hotels cater more to business travelers than to tourists, so prices and availability are a little better on Fridays and Saturdays.

There are only a few small, family-style hotels left in the center, and the good ones charge top dollar for their location. To save money, consider searching online for a deal at a basic chain hotel (such as Ibis) near a Metro stop.

MILAN

NEAR THE DUOMO

The Duomo area is thick with people-watching, reasonably priced eateries, and the major sightseeing attractions, but hotel prices are high.

$$$$ Hotel Spadari boasts a modern, Art Deco-inspired lobby designed by the Milanese artist Giò Pomodoro ("Joe Tomato" in English). The 40 rooms have billowing drapes, big paintings, and designer doors. It's next to the recommended Peck Gourmet Deli, and two blocks from the Duomo (RS%, air-con, elevator, Via Spadari 11, tel. 02-7200-2371, www.spadarihotel.com, reservation@spadarihotel.com).

$$$$ Hotel Gran Duca di York, three blocks from the Duomo, is on a stark street of banks and public buildings. Public areas are comfortable and spacious, and the 33 rooms are modern and bright (RS%, air-con, elevator, near Metro stops: Cordusio or Duomo, Via Moneta 1, tel. 02-874-863, www.ducadiyork.com, info@ducadiyork.com).

BETWEEN LA SCALA AND SFORZA CASTLE

These slightly-less-central places are close to the Via Dante and Via Brera shopping and restaurant scenes.

$$$$ Antica Locanda dei Mercanti offers 15 rooms in an 18th-century palazzo. While each room has its own personality (some have kitchenettes, others have small terraces), all have a fresh-flower vibe that embraces old and new—a nice change for businesslike Milan (RS%—use code "RSMILANO", air-con, elevator, Via San Tomaso 6, reception on first floor, Metro: Cairoli or Cordusio, tel. 02-805-4080, www.locanda.it, locanda@locanda.it, Alex and Eri).

$$$ Hotel Star rents 30 rooms, most of which have been modernized and feature artsy, somewhat gaudy decor; interior rooms are quieter (air-con, elevator, usually closes for 2 weeks mid-Aug, Via dei Bossi 5, Metro: Cordusio, tel. 02-801-501, www.hotelstar.it, hotelstar@hotelstar.it, Vittoria).

$$ London Hotel is a faded, old-school hotel with a living room-like lobby and 29 basic rooms with tiny bathrooms. It's overpriced for what you get, but in a fine location (cheaper rooms with shared bath, breakfast extra—better to grab something on Via Dante, air-con, elevator, Via Rovello 3, Metro: Cairoli, tel. 02-7202-0166, www.hotellondonmilano.com, info@hotellondonmilano.com, sisters Tanya and Licia).

NEAR *THE LAST SUPPER*

These two hotels are farther from the action in a sleepy, mostly residential zone, but the prices are lower.

$$$ Antica Locanda Leonardo, just down the street from

The Last Supper, has a romantic, Old World vibe and antique furnishings. Each of its 16 uniquely decorated rooms face either a courtyard (cheaper, some street noise) or a tranquil garden (RS%, some rooms with garden balcony, air-con, elevator, Corso Magenta 78, tel. 02-4801-4197, www.anticalocandaleonardo.com, info@anticalocandaleonardo.com). From the Duomo area, you can ride tram #16 or take the Metro to either Cadorna or Conciliazione and walk five minutes.

$$ B&B Hotel Milano Sant'Ambrogio, part of a chain of budget hotels, has 75 efficient, cookie-cutter rooms. They come with some tram noise (request a quieter one) but are worth considering if you can get a deal (breakfast extra, air-con, elevator, Via degli Olivetani 4, Metro: S. Ambrogio, tel. 02-4810-1089, www.hotelbb.com, mi.santambrogio@hotelbb.com). It's on a side street near the Leonardo da Vinci Science Museum, about a five-minute walk from either *The Last Supper* or Basilica Sant'Ambrogio.

NEAR MILANO CENTRALE TRAIN STATION

The train station neighborhood is more practical than characteristic. Its hotels are utilitarian business-class places with prices that bounce all over depending upon the convention schedule; most of the year, many have rooms in the €100-125 range. You'll find more shady characters than shady trees in the parks, and lots of ethnic restaurants and massage parlors as you head away from the immediate vicinity of the station. But it's convenient to trains, the Metro, and airport shuttles, and if you hit it outside of convention times, the prices are hard to beat.

On Via Napo Torriani: This street, a five-minute walk from the station, is lined with midrange hotels (exit the station, head straight across the square, then veer left onto Via Napo Torriani). **$$ Hotel Berna** feels like a classic European hotel, with an old-school lobby, uniformed bellhops, and 116 faded rooms with some nice upgrades (air-con, elevator, Via Napo Torriani 18, tel. 02-677-311, www.hotelberna.com). **$$ Hotel Garda** is cheaper and less welcoming, with 55 rooms (RS%—email first to get a promo code, then book on their website; breakfast extra, air-con, elevator, Via Napo Torriani 21, tel. 02-6698-2626, www.hotelgardamilan.com).

Hostel: ¢ Ostello Bello Grande has converted what was a business-class hotel into a well-priced hostel with hipster flair. Worth considering even if you're not a hosteler, it comes with an inviting rooftop terrace and a shared kitchen (private rooms available, includes breakfast and *aperitivo* happy-hour snacks, air-con, elevator, laundry, Via Lepetit 33, tel. 02-670-5921, www.ostellobello.com). With the tracks to your back, leave the station to the left, cross the taxi stand, and then cross the road. The hostel is around the corner from Ristorante Giglio Rosso.

MILAN

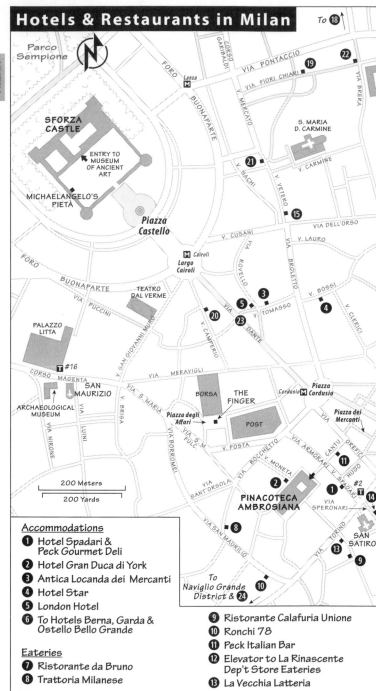

Hotels & Restaurants in Milan

To ⑱

Parco Sempione

FORO BUONAPARTE

CORSO GARIBALDI

VIA PONTACCIO ⑲

VIA FIORI CHIARI

VIA BRERA

⑫

Lanza Ⓜ

VIA MERCATO

S. MARIA D. CARMINE

SFORZA CASTLE

ENTRY TO MUSEUM OF ANCIENT ART

V. SACHI

㉑

V. CARMINE

V. VETERO

MICHAELANGELO'S PIETÀ

Piazza Castello

⑮

VIA DELL'ORSO

V. CUSANI

V. LAURO

FORO BUONAPARTE

Cairoli Ⓜ

Largo Cairoli

VIA ROVELLO

VIA BROLETTO

V. BOSSI

TEATRO DAL VERME

VIA PUCCINI

⑳

⑤ ③

V. TOMASSO

④

V. CLERICI

PALAZZO LITTA

V. SAN GIOVANNI MURO

V. CAMPERIO

㉓

VIA DANTE

CORSO MAGENTA

Ⓣ #16

VIA MERAVIGLI

Cordusio Ⓜ

Piazza Cordusio

SAN MAURIZIO

V. S MARIA

V. BRISA

BORSA

THE FINGER

Piazza dei Mercanti

ARCHAEOLOGICAL MUSEUM

VIA NIRONE

VIA LUINI

Piazza degli Affari

POST

VIA ARMORARI

CANTU

OREFICI

V. S. FUC

V. POSTA

V. S. HUGO

⑪

VIA BOCCHETTO

V. MONETA

②

①

#2 Ⓣ

VIA SANT'ORSOLA

VIA BORROMEI

PINACOTECA AMBROSIANA

VIA SPERONARI

⑭

200 Meters

200 Yards

VIA SAN MAURILIO

⑧

V. TORINO

⑬

SAN SATIRO

To Naviglio Grande District & ㉔

⑩

⑨

Accommodations
① Hotel Spadari & Peck Gourmet Deli
② Hotel Gran Duca di York
③ Antica Locanda dei Mercanti
④ Hotel Star
⑤ London Hotel
⑥ To Hotels Berna, Garda & Ostello Bello Grande

Eateries
⑦ Ristorante da Bruno
⑧ Trattoria Milanese

⑨ Ristorante Calafuria Unione
⑩ Ronchi 78
⑪ Peck Italian Bar
⑫ Elevator to La Rinascente Dep't Store Eateries
⑬ La Vecchia Latteria

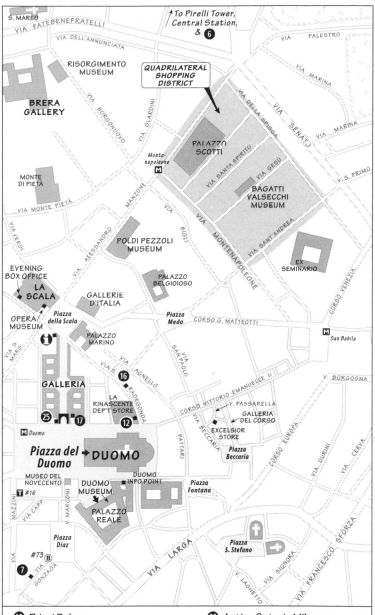

⑭ Princi Bakery	⑳ Antica Osteria Milanese
⑮ Princi Café	㉑ Convivium Ristorante & Pizza
⑯ Luini Panzerotti & Cioccolati Italiani	㉒ Bar Brera & Via Brera Eateries
⑰ Il Mercato del Duomo	㉓ Via Dante Eateries
⑱ To Eataly	㉔ To Naviglio Grande Eateries
⑲ Via Fiori Chiari Eateries	㉕ Bar Camparino

Eating in Milan

Milan's hundreds of trendy bars, delis, *rosticcerie,* and self-service cafeterias cater to people with plenty of taste and more money than time. You'll find delightful eateries all over town (note that many places close in August). To eat mediocre food on a street with great people-watching, choose an eatery on the pedestrian-only Via Dante. To eat with students in trendy little trattorias, explore the Brera neighborhood (especially the pedestrianized Via Fiori Chiari). To eat well near the Duomo, consider the recommended places listed later.

Some locals like to precede dinner with an *aperitivo*—a before-meal drink (while Campari made its debut in Milan, a simple glass of *vino bianco* or prosecco, the Italian champagne, is just as popular). At about 18:00, bars fill their counters with inviting baskets of munchies, served free with these drinks. If you're either likable or discreet, a cheap drink can become a light meal. This *aperitivo* custom is common throughout Italy but especially prized by the Milanesi—who claim they invented it.

Milan's signature dishes (often served together) are *risotto alla Milanese* and *ossobuco.* The risotto is flavored with saffron, which gives it an intense yellow color. The subtle flavor of the saffron pairs nicely with the veal shanks of *ossobuco* (meaning "marrow" or, literally, "hole in the bone" shank). The prized marrow, extracted with special little forks, is considered the best part of the meal. Also popular is the *cotoletta alla Milanese,* a thin, breaded veal cutlet fried in clarified butter. Some places have supersized it and call it *orecchio di elefante,* an "elephant's ear" (large enough to share).

NEAR THE DUOMO
Restaurants with Class
$$ Ristorante da Bruno, true to their family roots, serves Tuscan cuisine with a passion for fresh fish. A traditional-feeling place, it impresses with its dressy waiters, hearty food (including Milanese specialties), and a fine antipasti buffet. You can eat inside or on the sidewalk under fascist-style columns (daily 12:00-23:00, closed Aug, air-con, Via M. Gonzaga 6, reservations wise, tel. 02-804-364, www.ristorantedabruno.biz, Graziella).

$$$ Trattoria Milanese is family-run and traditional, on a dark back street. It has an enthusiastic clientele, with a sometimes-lukewarm staff—the restaurant didn't even bother to get a phone until 1988. Expect an old-fashioned Milanese ambience. Eat early for a less-crowded atmosphere (Mon-Sat 12:00-15:00 & 19:00-22:30, closed Sun and mid-July-Aug, evening reservations recommended, air-con, Via Santa Marta 11, near Pinacoteca Ambrosiana, tel. 02-8645-1991).

$$ Ristorante Calafuria Unione is a bustling, unpretentious place that attracts a sizable crowd for its pizza and traditional dishes. It feels like a well-loved neighborhood eatery (Mon-Sat 12:00-15:00 & 19:00-24:00, closed Sun, air-con, a few blocks south of Piazza del Duomo at Via dell'Unione 8, Metro: Missori, tel. 02-866-103).

$$$ Ronchi 78, a Milan institution for a century, is tight and atmospheric. The main dining room is cozy, while downstairs, more seating sprawls through vaulted cellars. Come here for traditional Milanese cuisine—and, if you're eating late like the Italians do, stay for the nightly "guitarroche" live music (cheaper at lunch, closed Sun, Via San Maurilio 7, tel. 02-867-295, www.ronchi78.it).

$$ Peck Italian Bar is a hit with the sophisticated office crowd, which mobs the place at lunch for its fast, excellent meals with im-peck-able service. It's owned by the same people who run the recommended high-end Peck Gourmet Deli (listed later), so be prepared to spend—getting to hang out and be part of the scene makes it worth the money. Any time you find yourself among such a quality-conscious group of Milanesi, you know you're getting good food (Mon-Fri 8:00-22:30, Sat from 9:00, closed Sun, Via Cantù 3, tel. 02-869-3017, www.peck.it).

Dining with a Duomo View

The seventh floor of La Rinascente department store, alongside the Duomo, has an upscale food court. Three of its many eateries share a sunny outdoor terrace with views of the cathedral's rooftop: **$$$ Obicà** is a swanky "mozzarella bar" (part of a chain), offering this heavenly cheese in all its various forms—cow's milk, buffalo, and smoked—in salads, on pizzas, or on splittable €23 antipasto sampler plates, accompanied by *salumi,* tapenades, and vegetables (there are dishes without mozzarella, too). **$$$ Ristorante Maio** has pricey full-meal service. And **$$$ Il Bar,** living-room cozy with cushy divans and low coffee tables, serves light meals (salads, pasta), coffee, desserts, and cocktails (all three open daily until 24:00; after store hours, use the elevator on Via S. Radegonda to enter).

Cheaper Eats and Takeout near the Duomo

$ La Vecchia Latteria, with a 50-year history, is a bright hole-in-the-wall that serves a good vegetarian lunch. This busy joint—with tight seating in front and behind the kitchen—serves soup, salads, pastas, and imaginative veggie entrées at affordable prices. Their star offering is *il misto forno,* a delicious assortment of soufflés, quiches, and roasted and sautéed veggies (Mon-Sat 12:00-16:00, closed Sun, just off Via Torino at Via dell'Unione 6, a few blocks southwest of the Duomo, Metro: Missori, tel. 02-874-401).

$ Princi bakery is mobbed with locals vying for focaccia, olive breadsticks, and luscious pastries. Notice the stacked-wood-oven action in the back. For most pastry items (like the brioche), pay the cashier first; for items sold by weight (such as pizza and cake), get it weighed before you pay. Consider a pasta lunch (12:00-15:00 only) for €7 per plate (open Mon-Sat 7:00-20:00, Sun 9:00-19:30; off Via Torino, a block southwest of Piazza del Duomo at Via Speronari 6; tel. 02-874-797). Another Princi bakery, more like a café, is near Sforza Castle and is listed later.

Peck Gourmet Deli is an aristocratic deli with a pricey gourmet grocery, *rosticceria,* and pastry/gelato shop on the main level; a fancy restaurant upstairs; and an expensive *enoteca* wine cellar in the basement. Even if all you can afford is the aroma, peek in. Check out the classic circa-1930 salami slicers and the gourmet assembly line in the kitchen in the back. The *rosticceria* serves delectable fancy food-to-go for a superb picnic dinner. It's sold by weight; order by the *etto*—100-gram unit, 250 grams equals about a half-pound (Mon 15:30-20:30, Tue-Fri 9:30-20:30, Sat 9:00-20:00, Sun 10:00-17:00, Via Spadari 9, tel. 02-802-3161).

$ Luini Panzerotti, a local institution, is a bakery that serves up €3 piping-hot mini calzones *(panzerotti)* stuffed with mozzarella, tomatoes, ham, or whatever you like (Mon 10:00-15:00, Tue-Sat until 20:00, closed Sun and Aug, Via S. Radegonda 16, tel. 02-8646-1917). From the back of the Duomo, head north and look for the lines out front. Order from the menus posted on the wall behind the cash registers. Traditionally, Milanesi munch their hot little meals on the benches of nearby Piazza San Fedele (just to the north). Don't overlook the *dolci* half of the menu. Across the street is another local hit, **Cioccolati Italiani,** for chocoholics in search of a treat.

Upscale Food Halls

Across from the Duomo, next to Galleria Vittorio Emanuele II, **Il Mercato del Duomo** has conquered several floors above La Feltrinelli bookstore. Budget options abound with a pasta bar, focaccia/sandwich section, "street food," and a *caffétteria.* Lighter fare is at their salad and *salumi* bar. For a fancy drink, head to the champagne bar or the Aperol terrace (daily 11:00-22:00, Piazza del Duomo 1, tel. 02-8633-1924, www.ilmercatodelduomo.it). And for a splurge, go to the top-floor restaurant Spazio Milano, run by three-star Michelin chef Niko Romito's cooking school (daily 12:30-14:30 & 19:30-22:00, www.nikoromitoformazione.it).

Similarly, **Eataly** (also in Rome, Florence, and New York) has turned the former Teatro Smeraldo into a gourmet megastore. It's overwhelming but oddly enchanting, with its overpriced Italian market goods and restaurants with all the major food groups—pasta, meats, vegetables, chocolate, and, of course, gelato (daily

10:00-24:00, Piazza XXV Aprile 10, Metro: Moscova, tel. 02-4949-7301, www.eataly.net).

EATING NEAR VIA BRERA AND VIA DANTE

These restaurants are near the Cairoli and Lanza Metro stations and are convenient to Sforza Castle and nearby recommended hotels. The Brera neighborhood, surrounding the Church of St. Carmine, is laced with narrow, inviting pedestrian streets. Make an evening of your visit by having an *aperitivo* with snacks at recommended Bar Brera or any other bar—most serve munchies with drinks from 17:00 until 21:00. Afterward, stroll along restaurant row on Via Fiori Chiari and Via Brera, or duck into the semicircular lane of Via Madonnina to survey the sidewalk cafés as you pass fortune tellers, artists, and knockoff handbag vendors.

$$ Antica Osteria Milanese is a hardworking family place with a smart local following and spacious, stylish seating. They serve good-quality, typical Milanese favorites (Mon-Sat 12:15-14:30 & 19:30-22:30, closed Sun, Via Camperio 12, tel. 02-861-367, Alessandro).

$$$ Convivium Ristorante and Pizza is popular for its extensive wine list, clever dishes (especially beef and fish), and tempting desserts. It's bustling and trendy, yet classy (daily 12:00-14:30 & 19:00-24:00, facing Santa Maria del Carmine church at Via Ponte Vetero 21, tel. 02-8646-3708, Claudio and Nicola).

$ Princi bakery's branch on Via Ponte Vetero works the same as the one on Via Speronari (listed earlier), only it's more like a restaurant, with seating both inside and on the street. While the bakery and café are open all day, their meal counter (with €7 plates) serves only from 12:00 to 15:00 (Mon-Sat 7:00-20:00, Sun from 9:00, Via Ponte Vetero 10, tel. 02-7201-6067).

$ Bar Brera serves inexpensive sandwiches, pastas, and salads to throngs of art students and has a lively *aperitivo* happy hour (drinks and a buffet of hearty snacks starts at 18:00; open daily 7:00-late, Via Brera 23, tel. 02 877 091).

Fancy Via Dante Bars and Cafés: Thriving and central, Via Dante is lined with hardworking eateries where you can join locals for a lively lunch. Or just swing by for a morning *caffè*, watching the parade of Milanesi heading to work.

IN NAVIGLIO GRANDE (CANAL DISTRICT)

Consider ending your day at the former port of Milan. The Naviglio Grande district bustles with memorable and affordable bars and restaurants and a great people scene. In addition to endless *aperitivo* spreads and traditional trattorias, there are some more creative choices, too: Greek fare, artisanal microbrews, and "Brazilian sushi."

Getting There: Ride the Metro or tram #2 to Porta Genova and walk down Via Casale, which dead-ends a block away at the canal. Walk halfway across the metal bridge and survey the scene. The street you just walked has plenty of cheap options. Most of the action—and all of my other recommendations—are to the left, on or near the canal. Do a reconnaissance stroll before settling in somewhere: Walk down the left bank of the canal to the bridge with cars, then go back on the other side.

Here are a few good options to consider, listed in the order you'll pass them.

$$$$ Ristorante Brellin is the top romantic splurge, with a dressy crowd and fine food. The menu is international while clinging to a bit of tradition (daily 12:30-15:00 & 19:00-23:00; located where a small lane, Vicolo dei Lavandai, branches off from the canal; tel. 02-5810-1351, www.brellin.it).

$ Pizzeria Tradizionale, at the far end of the walk after you cross the bridge, is a local favorite (Thu-Tue 12:00-14:30 & 19:00-24:00, Wed 19:00-24:00, at the far end of canal walk, Ripa di Porta Ticinese 7, tel. 02-839-5133).

$$ Cucina Fusetti is a charming little place a few doors off the canal, serving pan-Mediterranean cuisine, including *bacalao*—salt cod (Mon-Sat 19:00-23:00, closed Sun; near the curved bridge with the zigzag design, go away from canal on Via Argelati to Via M. Fusetti 1; mobile 340-861-2676).

$ Pizzeria Spaghetteria La Magolfa, down a side street, feels like a neighborhood hangout, offering good, cheap salads, pastas, and pizzas. You can sit inside, on a veranda, or at a table on the street. For less than €20, two people could split a hearty pizza and a good bottle of wine (daily 12:00-15:00 & 18:00-24:00, go a long block past Cucina Fusetti to end of street, Via Magolfa 15, tel. 02-832-1696.

On your way back to the Metro or tram, stop by **Orso Bianco** for "artisanal" gelato. Their *nocciola*—or hazelnut—is *buonissimo* (Via Casale 7, on your right as you walk back to the Metro, tel. 02-9738-6848).

Milan Connections

BY TRAIN

From Milano Centrale to: Venice (2/hour, most direct on high-speed ES trains, 2.5 hours), **Florence** (Trenitalia: hourly, 2 hours; Italo: 2/hour, 2 hours), **Genoa** (hourly, 2 hours), **Rome** (Trenitalia: 1-3/hour, 3.5 hours; Italo: 11/day nonstop, 3 hours, more with stops), **Brindisi** (4 direct/day, 2 night trains, 9-15 hours), **Cinque Terre/La Spezia** (hourly, 3 hours direct or with change in Genoa; trains from La Spezia to the villages go nearly hourly), **Cinque Terre/Monterosso al Mare** (8/day direct, otherwise hourly with change in Genoa, 3 hours), **Varenna** on Lake Como (1 hour; small line direct to Lecco/

Sondrio/Tirano leaves at :20 past most hours—confirm these times), **Stresa** on Lake Maggiore (about hourly; 50-minute fast train may require reservations, while 1.5-hour train doesn't), **Como** (2/hour, 30-60 minutes, boats go from Como to Varenna until about 19:00), **Naples** (Trenitalia: 2/hour, 4-5 hours, more with change in Rome, overnight possible; Italo: 11/day, 4-5 hours). For details see www.trenitalia.com or www.italotreno.it.

From Milano Porta Garibaldi (by High-Speed Train to International Destinations): **Basel,** with connections to Frankfurt (3/day, 4 hours), **Geneva** (4/day, 4 hours), **Lugano** (almost hourly, 1 hour), **Munich** (night train, 12 hours), **Nice** (3/day direct, 5 hours, operated by Thello, no rail passes; more with changes via Trenitalia), **Paris** (3/day, 7 hours; daily night train from Milano Centrale, 11 hours, operated by Thello, no rail passes), **Vienna** (night train, 12 hours), **Zürich** (4/day, 3 hours).

BY PLANE

To get flight information for Malpensa or Linate airports or the phone number of your airline, call 02-74851 or 02-232-323 and wait for English options, or check www.sea-aeroportimilano.it.

Note: While the train works best for Malpensa, if you want to take a shuttle bus to any of Milan's airports, just go to Milano Centrale station and walk out the door marked *Piazza Luigi di Savoia.* There, you'll find little sales kiosks aggressively selling tickets for all your options.

Malpensa Airport

Most international flights land at Terminal 1 of the manageable Malpensa Airport (airport code: MXP), 28 miles northwest of Milan. Low-cost EU flights use Terminal 2 (buses connect the two). Both have ATMs and exchange offices. Terminal 1 has a pharmacy, eateries, and a hotel-reservation service disguised as a TI. To leave the baggage-carousel area A, go right to reach services and the exit. From area B, go left. Airport info: Tel. 02-5858-0080, www.milanomalpensa-airport.com.

Trains from Malpensa to Milan: The Malpensa Express train is usually the most sensible option (not covered by rail passes, tel. 800-500-005, www.malpensaexpress.it). Trains leave from underground stations at Terminals 1 and 2. To reach the Terminal 2 station, exit the arrivals hall, cross the street, and follow the covered walkway to the station entrance. Both stations have ticket offices and Trenord ticket machines (credit cards accepted). A big electronic board shows the next departure times (*"bin"* = track). There are two lines: Malpensa-Milano Cadorna and Malpensa-Milano Centrale. For either, the ride costs €13 one-way (€20 round-trip).

MILAN

Train Connections from Milan

Note: In addition to regular rail, Milan is connected to Venice, Bologna, Florence, Rome, Naples, and Turin via high-speed rail.

Rail — — Bus

30 Kilometers

30 Miles

Validate your ticket in the little machines, and double-check to make sure your train is going to the destination you want.

If you are headed downtown or to most other points in the city, take the **Cadorna** line, which is quicker, runs more often and later, and drops you at a convenient downtown Metro station (2/hour, 40 minutes, usually departs Terminal 2 at :20 and :50 past the hour—departs Terminal 1 about 6 minutes later, last train from airport leaves at 1:03 in the morning; returning from Cadorna to the airport, the train generally departs Cadorna at :27 and :57 past the hour, first train from Cadorna leaves at 4:27).

If you are heading to the area around Milano Centrale, or connecting by train to other destinations, take the **Centrale** line (2/hour, 50 minutes, usually departs Terminal 2 at :07 and :37 past the hour—departs Terminal 1 about 6 minutes later, last train from airport leaves at 22:43; returning from Milano Centrale to the airport, the train generally departs at :25 and :55 past the hour, first train from Milano Centrale leaves at 5:25).

If you're **leaving Milan** to go *to* the airport, purchase your ticket before you board, either from the Trenitalia or Trenord ticket machines or, at Cadorna Station, from the staffed ticket windows. At Milano Centrale, trains usually leave from tracks 1 and 2, which are hidden behind tracks 3 and 4 and poorly signed. Cadorna is a little easier to deal with; trains usually depart from track 1.

By Shuttle Bus: Three bus companies run between Malpensa Airport and Milano Centrale train station, offering virtually identical, competing services. They each charge about €8 for the one-hour trip (buy ticket from driver) and depart from the same places: in front of Terminal 2 (outside exit 4) and from Piazza Luigi di Savoia (on the east side of Milan's central train station—with your back to the tracks, exit to the left). They also pick up and drop off at Terminal 1, which, if your flight docks there, makes the bus an option rather than taking the train. Buses leave about every 20 minutes, every day, from very early until just after midnight (Malpensa Shuttle tel. 02-5858-3185, www.malpensashuttle.it; Autostradale tel. 02-3391-0794, www.autostradale.it; and Terravision, www.terravision.eu).

By Taxi: Taxis into Milan cost a fixed rate of €95; avoid hustlers in airport halls (catch taxis outside exit 8). Considering how far the city is from the airport and how good the train and bus services are, Milan is the last place I'd take an airport taxi.

Linate Airport
Most European flights land at Linate (airport code: LIN, www.milanolinate-airport.com), five miles east of Milan. The airport has a bank with an ATM (just past customs) and a hotel-finding service disguised as a TI (daily 7:30-23:30, tel. 02-7020-0443). Eventually the Metro's new line 4 will link Linate with the city. For now, you can get to downtown Milan by bus or taxi.

By Bus: Public bus #73 connects Linate to the Duomo in about 25 minutes (covered by €1.50 public transit ticket, departs every 10 minutes, less frequently evenings and Sun).

If you're *leaving* Milan to go to the airport, look for the #73 bus stop near the Duomo—it's just off Piazza Armando Diaz where it meets Via Maurizio Gonzaga.

Private companies also run shuttles to Milano Centrale train station (handy only if you're catching a train; €5, 2/hour, 35 minutes, www.airportbusexpress.it).

By Taxi: Taxis from Linate to the Duomo cost about €25.

Bergamo (Orio al Serio) Airport
Some budget airlines, such as Ryanair and Wizz Air, use Bergamo Airport—about 30 miles from Milan—as their Milan hub (airport code: BGY, tel. 035-326-323, www.sacbo.it). At least three bus companies ply the route between the east side of Milano Centrale train station (Piazza Luigi di Savoia) and Orio al Serio (€5, about 5/hour, 1 hour): Autostradale (www.airportbusexpress.it), Terravision (www.terravision.eu), and the Orio Shuttle (www.orioshuttle.com).

THE LAKES

Commune with nature where Italy is joined to the Alps, in the lovely Italian lakes district. In this land of lakes, the million-euro question is: Which one? For the best mix of accessibility, scenery, and offbeatness, the village of Varenna on Lake Como is my top choice, while Lake Maggiore is a suitable backup. In either place, you'll get a complete dose of Italian-lakes wonder and aristocratic-old-days romance.

You could spend a busy day side-tripping from Milan (about one hour away by train) to either lake, do some island- and villa-hopping, and be home in time for dinner. But the lakes are an ideal place to slow down and take a break from your busy vacation. Settle in here, and bustling Milan doesn't even exist. Now it's your turn to be *chiuso per restauro* (closed for restoration). If relaxation's not on your agenda, the lakes shouldn't be either.

Lake Como

Lake Como (Lago di Como)—lined with elegant 19th-century villas, crowned by snowcapped mountains, and busy with ferries, hydrofoils, and slow, passenger-only boats—is a good place to take a break from the intensity and turnstile culture of central Italy. It seems like half the travelers you'll meet have tossed their itineraries into the lake and are actually relaxing.

Lake Como is Milan's quick getaway, and the sleepy mid-lake village of Varenna is the handiest base of operations. With good connections to other mid-lake towns (and Milan), Varenna is my

favorite place to stay on the lake. While Varenna has a village vibe, beautiful Bellagio has earned its ritzy allure and feels a bit more like a real city, making it a good alternative.

The hazy, lazy lake's only serious industry is tourism. Every day, hundreds of lakeside residents commute to work in Lugano, just across the border in Switzerland. The lake's isolation and flat economy have left it pretty much the way the 19th-century Romantic poets described it: heaven on earth.

PLANNING YOUR TIME

Even though there are no essential activities, plan for at least two nights so you'll have an uninterrupted day to see how slow you can get your pulse. Spend some time exploring your home-base town, take my self-guided ferry tour to take in the scenery (with visits to the lake's two main villas), and hop off the boat to poke around the town you're not staying in. With additional time, visit more lakeside villas or go for a hike.

Lake Como is also workable as a day trip from Milan. Take a morning train to Varenna, ride the boat to Lenno (and tour Villa

Balbianello), then take a boat to Villa Carlotta to tour the gardens. From there, head either to Bellagio or back to Varenna to linger and explore (or, with more time and energy, see a little of both) before taking the train back to Milan from Varenna. Start early to pack everything in; otherwise, you'll have to be more selective (with time to see just one of the villas).

GETTING TO LAKE COMO

By Train via Varenna: From any destination covered in this book, you'll reach Lake Como via Milan. The quickest, easiest, and cheapest way to get from Milan to any mid-lake town is to take the train to Varenna. From Varenna you can hop on a boat to Bellagio.

At Milano Centrale train station, catch a train heading for Sondrio or Tirano—sometimes the departure board also says "Lecco/Tirano." (Tirano is often confused with Torino...wrong city.) All Sondrio-bound trains stop in Varenna, as noted in the fine print on the *partenze* (departures) schedule posted at Milan's train station. Trains leave Milan nearly hourly at :20 past the hour, with a few two-hour gaps (confirm times at station or online at www.trenitalia.com). Get a second-class ticket, since most of these trains don't have first-class cars (rail passes accepted). If you plan to head back to Milan on the train, also buy a return ticket. Stamp your ticket in the yellow box or risk a €50 fine. If you run into a problem or need to validate your rail pass at Milan's train station, find the helpful Trenitalia office on the ground floor.

Leaving Milan, sit on the left for maximum lake-view beauty. Get off at Varenna-Esino-Perledo. (Even though train schedules list just Varenna or Varenna-Esino, Varenna-Esino-Perledo is what you'll see at the platform.) The long trains that serve Varenna's tiny station stop only briefly—be ready to hop out. The single platform is very narrow, and your car may actually stop before or after the platform. Look out the window. If even part of the train is at the station, you'll need to get out and walk. Tips: Board midtrain to land next to a platform. Leave from the door through which you entered, since you know it's working. If necessary, pull hard on the red handle (or push the button) to open the door.

By Train and Boat via Como: For a less convenient, much slower, but more scenic trip, you can get to Varenna or Bellagio from Milan via the town of Como. Trains take you from Milan to Como (2/hour, 30-60 minutes). From the station in Como, it's a 10-minute walk to the dock, where you catch either the speedy hydrofoil or the leisurely *battello* (slow boat—great for enjoying the scenery) for the ride up the lake to Bellagio or Varenna. Boats leave Como about every 2 hours (*battello:* €11.60, 2.5 hours, last departure about 15:20; hydrofoil: €16.20, 1 hour, last departure about 19:20, fewer on Sun, www.navigazionelaghi.it).

Boat Schedule Literacy

Types of Boats
Traghetto or *autotraghetto:* Car and passenger ferry
Aliscafo or *servizio rapido:* Hydrofoil (pricier, faster, enclosed, and less scenic)
Battello ship: Slow passenger-only boat going all the way to Como
Battello navetta: Shuttle serving mid-lake only

Schedule Terms
Feriali: Monday-Saturday
Festivi: Sundays and holidays
Partenze da...: Departing from...

By Plane via Milan's Airports: Take the Malpensa Express train from Malpensa Airport, the Airport Bus Express from Linate Airport, or any of the buses from Bergamo's Orio al Serio Airport to Milano Centrale train station, and then transfer to a Varenna-bound train (see earlier).

By Taxi: Taxis between Varenna and Milan or its airports won't save money over the train, even for groups, but can be worth it for the convenience. **Marco Barili** (and his wife Nelly) don't charge extra for baggage or early/late departures (€150 to central Milan or Linate Airport for up to 4 people/€200 for 5-8 people in a minibus, €160/€220 to Malpensa Airport, €130/€180 to Orio al Serio Airport, tel. 0341-815-061, taxi.varenna@tiscali.it).

GETTING AROUND LAKE COMO

By Boat: Boats go about every 30 minutes between Varenna and Bellagio (€4.60/hop, cash only, 15-20 minutes, daily approximately

7:00-22:30). If you're staying in one of these towns, you'll probably limit your cruising to this scenic mid-lake area. Express boats cost a little more and save only a couple of minutes per leg. Because boats are frequent and the schedule is hard to read, I just show up, buy a ticket for the next boat, and wait. Always ask which slip *(pontile)* your boat will leave from—it's not posted, and Bellagio has several docks (boat info: toll-free tel. 800-551-801 or tel. 031-579-211, www.navigazionelaghi.it). On sunny days, long lines can form at ticket booths; don't dillydally, and consider buying your tickets in advance at a quieter time. The one-day €15 mid-lake pass makes

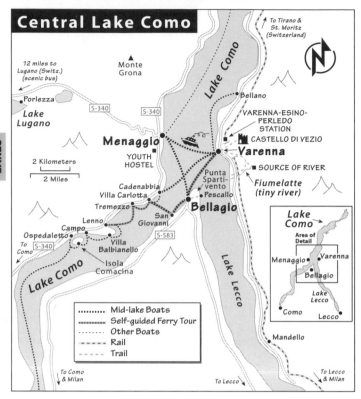

Central Lake Como

To Tirano &
St. Moritz
(Switzerland)

Lake Como

N

12 miles to
Lugano (Switz.)
(scenic bus)

Monte
Grona

Porlezza

Lake
Lugano

S-340

S-340

Bellano

VARENNA-ESINO-
PERLEDO
STATION

Menaggio

YOUTH
HOSTEL

CASTELLO DI VEZIO

Varenna

2 Kilometers

2 Miles

Punta
Sparti-
vento

SOURCE OF RIVER

Fiumelatte
(tiny river)

Cadenabbia
Villa Carlotta

Pescallo

Tremezzo

San
Giovanni

Bellagio

Lake
Como

Area of
Detail

Lenno

Campo

Ospedaletto

S-583

Menaggio

Varenna

To
Como

S-340

Villa
Balbianello

Bellagio

Isola
Comacina

Lake Como

Lake
Lecco

Lake Lecco

.... Mid-lake Boats

Como

Lecco

‒‒‒‒‒‒ Self-guided Ferry Tour

.... Other Boats

Mandello

+‒+‒+‒ Rail

‒ ‒ ‒ Trail

To Como
& Milan

To Lecco

To Lecco
& Milan

LAKES

sense only if you take four or more rides—unlikely (pass does not cover fast hydrofoils).

If you're making more complex plans, pick up a free **boat schedule** and ask for help to decipher it. It's a good idea to ask your hotelier to review your possible connections before you set out so you can pace your day smartly. You'll find the schedule at travel agencies, hotels, and boat docks. Confusingly, the schedule requires you to scan four different timetables to know all the departures; for key terms, see the sidebar.

By Car: With scarce parking, traffic jams, and expensive car ferries, this is no place to drive. While it's possible to drive around the lake, the road is narrow, congested, and lined with privacy-seeking walls, hedges, and tall fences. Parking in Bellagio is more difficult than in Varenna. If you do have a car, park it in Varenna, and use the boat to get around.

While you can rent cars in Bellagio, for most travelers, it's best to take the train to Milan and pick up a car there, either at the central train station or at one of Milan's three airports.

Varenna

This well-manicured village of 800 people offers the best of all lake worlds. Easily accessible by train, on the less-driven side of the lake, Varenna has a romantic  promenade, a tiny harbor, steep and narrow stepped lanes, and some scenic sights (a ruined castle and two villas). It's just the right place to savor a lakeside cappuccino or *aperitivo*. There's wonderfully little to do here, and it's very quiet at night...unless you're here during one of the hundred-or-so annual American wedding parties. The *passerella* (lakeside promenade, well-lit and inviting after dark) is adorned with caryatid lovers pressing silently against each other in the shadows. Varenna is a popular destination with my readers and European vacationers—book well in advance for high season (May-Oct). From November to mid-March, Varenna practically shuts down: Hotels close for the winter, and restaurants and shops reduce their hours.

Orientation to Varenna

TOURIST INFORMATION

The TI is near the **main square** (June-Sept daily 10:00-13:00 & 15:00-18:30; April-May and Oct Tue-Sat 10:00-12:30 & 14:30-18:00, Sun 10:00-12:30, closed Mon; weekends only Nov-March; just past the bank at Via IV Novembre 7, tel. 0341-830-367, www.varennaturismo.com). The Tivano travel agency, located in the **train station,** also operates as a TI (see "Helpful Hints"). At either TI (or your hotel), pick up the *Varenna Tourist Info* booklet.

ARRIVAL IN VARENNA

Varenna is small, and pretty much everything is within a 15-minute walk.

By Train: From Varenna's train station, you can **walk** along the marked pedestrian lane down to the main road. If you're heading for the ferry to Bellagio, go straight; otherwise, turn left along the main road and keep rolling into town (a 15-minute walk from the station; watch for traffic where the sidewalk ends). If you have a bag with wheels, avoid using the lakeside promenade, which ends in stairs and cobbles.

A **taxi** from the station costs about €10. Reliable Marco Barili (or his wife Nelly) can meet you at the train station if you know

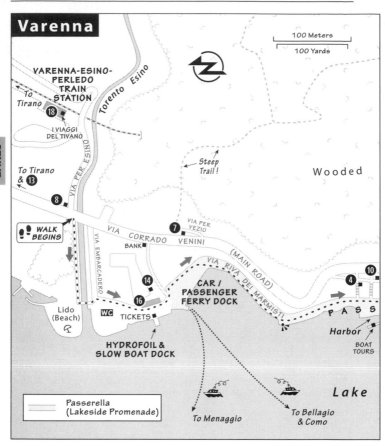

your exact arrival time. Look for a flashing sign with your name on it (tel. 0341-815-061, taxi.varenna@tiscali.it).

By Boat: The boat dock is close to the train station and a 10-minute stroll north of the main square and old town.

By Car: Avoid on-street parking in Varenna; the few spots are mostly reserved for residents. The easiest (though most expensive) parking option is the spiffy multilevel lot at the south end of town, across from the entrance to Villa Monastero (€2/hour 6:00-22:00, otherwise €1/hour, €20/24 hours).

Parking at the train station is free overnight, but you'll have to pay from 8:00 to 23:00 most of the year (€1.50/hour, feed coins into meter in center of lot and put ticket on dashboard; €15 day pass available from I Viaggi del Tivano travel agency or Café III Binario at the station).

LAKES

Accommodations
1. Hotel du Lac
2. Villa Cipressi & Ristorante la Contrada
3. Hotel Royal Victoria
4. Albergo Milano, Casa Rossa & Ristorante la Vista
5. To Hotel Eremo Gaudio
6. Albergo/Ristorante del Sole
7. Hotel Montecodeno
8. Albergo Beretta

Eateries & Other
9. Ristorante il Cavatappi
10. Osteria Quatro Pass
11. Varenna Monamour
12. Nilus Bar & Bar Il Molo
13. To Ristorante il Caminetto & Cooking Course
14. Pub l'Orso
15. Vecchia Varenna
16. Hotel/Ristorante Olivedo
17. Gelateria Riva & La Passerella
18. Café III Binario
19. Grocery (2)
20. Laundry (3)
21. Barilott Bar (Train Tickets)

HELPFUL HINTS

Travel Agency: Varenna's travel agency, **I Viaggi del Tivano,** is conveniently located in the train station. In addition to acting as a TI, they book planes, trains, and automobiles (Mon-Fri 9:00-13:00 & 14:30-18:30, Sat-Sun 9:00-16:00, Oct-April Sat until 13:00 and closed Sun; good place to pick up boat schedules, no service charge for regional train tickets, €5 booking fee for long-distance train tickets, tel. 0341-814-009, www.tivanotours.com, info@tivanotours.com, helpful Cristina and Eleonora). They also offer half-day and daylong bus and boat tours of the region, including Switzerland (April-Sept only, book tours by noon the day before).

Train Tickets: The train station doesn't have ticket windows, but you can buy tickets at the **I Viaggi del Tivano** travel agency there (see above). Don't cut it too close, in case there's a line. You can also buy tickets at the **Barilott** bar/tobacco shop downtown, which is also a lively place to buy a *panino* and/or a glass of wine and use the Wi-Fi (daily 7:00-20:00, closed Sun Oct-April, Via IV Novembre 6, tel. 0341-815-045, Claudia and Fabrizio).

Money: One bank is near Varenna's main square; another is located inland from the boat dock. Both have ATMs (see the Varenna map).

Post Office: It's at the bottom corner of the main square (Tue and Thu-Fri 8:20-13:45, Sat until 12:45).

Laundry: Lavanderia Pensa Barbara can wash and dry your laundry within 24 hours (priced by weight, no self-service, Mon-Fri 9:00-12:00 & 15:00-19:00, Sat 9:00-12:00, closed Sun, Via Venini 31, tel. 0341-830-478). A self-service machine is tucked in the back of the little **"Il Bottaio"** shopping gallery facing the harbor (€1 entry voucher covers WC or can be used toward food or drinks at nearby Bar Il Molo, daily 8:00-24:00). Another self-service option is just off the **main square,** between the recommended Albergo del Sole and the post office (daily 24 hours, Contrada del Prato 10).

Varenna Walk

Since you came here to relax, this short self-guided walk gives you just the town basics.

• *Begin by standing in the little piazza next to the…*

Bridge Just Below Train Station: This main bridge spans the tiny Esino River, which divides two communities: Perledo (which sprawls up the hill—notice the church spire high above) and the old fishing town of Varenna (huddled around its harbor). The train station, called Varenna-Esino-Perledo, gives due respect to both, as well as the village of Esino, eight miles higher in the hills.

Go down the tree-lined promenade on the right (north) side of the river. You'll run into the entrance to the town's public beach—the *lido* (small fee to enter)—and then cross the cute pedestrian bridge to the small square, which hosts a market on Wednesdays.

The yellow inn facing the ferry dock, Hotel Olivedo, has greeted ferry travelers since the 19th century and is named for the olive groves you can see growing halfway up the hill. Natives claim this is the farthest north that olives grow in Europe.

• *Across from Hotel Olivedo is Varenna's…*

Ferry Landing: Since the coming of the train in 1892, this has been the main link to Milan and the world for the "mid-lake" communities of Bellagio, Menaggio (described later), and Varenna. From this viewpoint, you can almost see how Lake Como is shaped like a man. The head is the north end (to the right, up by the Swiss Alps). Varenna is the left hip (to the east). Menaggio, across the lake, is the right hip (to the west). And Bellagio (hiding behind the smaller wooded hill to your left) is the crotch—or, more poetically, Punta Spartivento ("Point that Divides the Wind"). In a more colorful description, a traditional poem says, "Lake Como is a man, with Colico the head, Lecco and Como the feet, and Bellagio the testicles." (In the regional dialect, this rhymes—ask a native to say it for you.)

The farthest ridges high above the right hip mark the border of Switzerland. This region's longtime poverty shaped the local character (much like the Great Depression shaped the outlook of a generation of Americans). Many still remember that the Varenna side of the lake was the poorest, because those on the Menaggio side controlled the lucrative cigarette-smuggling business over the Swiss border. Today, the entire region is thriving—thanks to tourism.

• *Walk past the ferry dock and the small playground to Varenna's elevated shoreline walk, called the...*

Passerella: A generation ago, Varenna built this elegant lakeside promenade, which connects the ferry dock with the old town center. Strolling this lane, you'll come to the tiny, two-dinghy, concrete breakwater of a villa. Lake Como is lined with swanky 19th-century villas; their front doors face the lake to welcome visitors arriving by boat. At this point, the modern *passerella* cuts between  this villa's water gate and its private harbor. Just around the bend, enjoy a good Varenna town view. These buildings are stringently protected by preservation laws; you can't even change the color of your villa's paint.

Just over the hump (which allows boats into a covered moorage), look back and up at another typical old villa—with a private *passerella*, a lovely veil of wisteria, and a prime lakeview terrace. Many of these villas are owned by the region's "impoverished nobility." Bred and raised not to work, eventually they were unable to pay for the upkeep of their sprawling houses. Some of these villas have now been bought by the region's nouveau riche.

• *At the community harbor, walk to the end of the pier for a town overview, then continue under the old-time arcades toward the multihued homes facing the harbor.*

Varenna Harborfront: There are no streets in the old town—just the characteristic stepped lanes called *contrade*. Varenna was originally a fishing community. Even today, old-timers enjoy Lake

Como's counterpart to Nor-
wegian lutefisk: *missoltino*, air-
dried and salted lake "sardines."

Imagine the harbor 200
years ago—busy with coopers
fitting chestnut and oak staves
into barrels, stoneworkers carving the black marble that was
quarried just above town, and
fishermen dragging boats onto
the sloping beach. The little

stone harbor dates from about 1600. Today, the fishing boats are
just for recreation, and residents gather here with their kids to relax
by the lake.

At the south end of the harbor (in front of the recommended
Bar Il Molo), belly up to the banister of the terrace for a colorful
town view. Another traditional ditty goes, "If you love Lake Como,
you know Bellagio is the pearl...but Varenna is the diamond."

• *Continue straight, leaving the harbor. A lane curves around Hotel du
Lac (its fine lakeside terrace welcomes even nonguests for a drink), finishing with an unexpected hill. Finally you'll reach the tiny pebbly town
beach below. From here, climb the stairs and go through the yellow arch
to the square called...*

Piazza San Giorgio: Several churches face Varenna's town
square. The main church (Chiesa di San Giorgio) dates from the
13th century. Romantic Varenna is an understandably popular spot
for weddings—rice often litters the church's front yard. Stepping
inside, you'll find a few humble but centuries-old bits of carving
and frescoes. The black floor and chapels are made from the local
marble.

Just past the church and the municipal building is the TI and
the Ornithology and Natural Science Museum, with a small collection of stuffed birds and other wildlife (small fee to enter, same
hours as TI).

The Hotel Royal Victoria, also on the main square, recalls the
1839 visit of Queen Victoria, who registered herself as the Count-
ess of Clare in an attempt to remain anonymous.

The trees in the square are planted to make a V for Varenna.
The street plan survives from Roman times, when gutters flowed
down to the lake. The little church on the lake side of the square is
the baptistery. Dating from the ninth century, it's one of the oldest
churches on the lake, but is rarely open for visits.

Our walk is over. Facing the church, you can head right to
visit the gardens or to take a demanding hike up to the castle (both
described next, under "Sights and Activities in Varenna"). You can
go left to get to the train station or ferry dock—or for a less-de-

manding but still steep hike to the castle. Head back downhill to enjoy the beach (take either of the lanes flanking the Hotel Royal Victoria down to the water).

Sights and Activities in Varenna

▲Hike to Vezio Castle (Castello di Vezio)

A steep and stony trail leads to Varenna's ruined hilltop castle, located in the peaceful, traffic-free, one-chapel hamlet of Vezio. Take the small road, Via per Vezio (about 100 feet south of—and to the right of—Hotel Montecodeno), and figure on a 20-minute walk one-way. Arriving in Vezio, follow *castello* signs. You'll reach a bar (with drinks, light food, and WCs) that serves as the castle's ticket desk. Once inside the grounds, the views are the main attraction: Follow the little loop trail on the lake side of the castle for vistas down on Varenna's rooftops and the adjacent lakefront community of Pino. The castle itself is barren—a courtyard protecting an empty tower, where you can cross a drawbridge and climb 62 rickety wooden steps to earn 360 degrees of Lake Como panoramas.

Cost and Hours: €4, Mon-Fri 10:00-18:00, Sat-Sun 10:00-19:00, June-Aug stays open one hour later, March and Oct closes one hour earlier, closed Nov-Feb and in bad weather, mobile 333-448-5975, www.castellodivezio.it, Nicola.

Falconry Shows: The castle hosts low-key falconry shows, usually around 15:30—but check the website or call in the morning for times.

Hiking Back Down: You can hike back the way you came or make a loop by continuing down to the east end of Varenna, on a steeper, narrower, less-manicured trail. From the castle gate, turn right and follow signs for *Varenna Scabium* and *Sentiero del Viandante.* You'll wander past some backyards and some scenic tennis courts, then start to gradually descend, popping out at the parking garage for the Hotel Eremo Gaudio. From here, head down to the right to walk back into Varenna, passing the entrances for both Villa Monastero and Villa Cipressi (described next) on your way to the main square.

Gardens

Two separate manicured lakeside gardens sit next door to each other just a short distance from the main square. First are the small but lush terraces of **Villa Cipressi;** just beyond are the more interesting, open grounds of **Villa Monastero,** which also admits visitors into the former residence of the De Marchi

family, now a museum filled with overly ornate furnishings from the late 1800s. It's the handiest look inside one of the old villas that line the lakeshore, but the lack of information makes the place feel sterile. While the villas and gardens elsewhere on the lake are more magnificent (see "More Sights on Lake Como," later), these are a sufficient substitute if you're staying around Varenna.

Cost and Hours: Villa Cipressi—€5, daily 8:00-sunset, closed Dec-April, www.hotelvillacipressi.it; Villa Monastero— gardens-€5, gardens and museum-€8; gardens open daily 9:30-19:00, closed Nov-Feb; museum open Fri-Sun 9:30-19:00, closed Mon-Thu—except open daily in Aug, closed Nov-Feb; bar in garden serves snacks, tel. 0341-295-450, www.villamonastero.eu.

Nearby: The **Sala De Marchi,** across the street from the Villa Monastero entrance, hosts a different exhibition each month through the summer. Ask at the TI or check the posters to see what's on.

Swimming

There are three spots to swim in Varenna: the free little beach behind the Hotel Royal Victoria off Piazza San Giorgio, the central lakefront area by Nilus Bar, and the *lido.* The *lido* is by far the best-equipped for swimmers. Just north of the boat dock, it's essentially a wide concrete slab with sand and a swimming area off an old boat ramp. It has showers, bathrooms, a restaurant, a bar, and lounge chairs and umbrellas for rent (€2 entry, tel. 0341-815-3700). Swimming by the boat dock is strictly forbidden for safety reasons.

Boating

Taxi Boat Varenna organizes hour-long central lake tours (€30/ person), plus a 2.5-hour version that adds a stop at Villa Balbianello (€55/person, price includes villa entry and one-hour tour). They also offer hour-long romantic private tours (€160 for up to 6 people). Ask Luca about his special 3-hour "Tour George." Book directly on the website (mid-March-mid-Nov only, mobile 349-229-0953, www.taxiboatvarenna.com, info@taxiboatvarenna.com). A similar company works out of Bellagio.

If you want to be your own skipper, **Boats2rent** is a good option. They offer 40-horsepower motor boats (from €60/hour, up to six people, no license required but €100 and ID needed for deposit) and zero-horsepower kayaks (€10/hour) from the harbor in front of the Nilus Bar (tel. 348-347-2093, www.boats2rent-varenna.net).

Hiking

The town of **Fiumelatte,** about a half-mile south of Varenna, was named for its "milky river." Promoted as the shortest river in Italy (at 800 feet), it runs—like most of the area's tourist industry—only from April through September (though even then it may be dry, depending on the weather). The *La Sorgente del Fiumelatte* brochure, available at Varenna's TI, lays out a walk from Varenna to the Fiumelatte, then to the castle, and back. It's a 30-minute hike to the source *(sorgente)* of the river (at Varenna's monastery, take the high road, drop into the tranquil and evocative cemetery, and climb steps to the wooded trail leading to the peaceful and refreshing cave from which the river spouts).

For a longer hike in the opposite direction with lake views, ask the TI about the **Wayfarers' Path** (hike one-way up the lake, about 2-2.5 hours, not quite as steep as Fiumelatte hike). You can return by train or boat from Bellano (check schedule before you go).

Cooking Course

Charming chef Moreno of the recommended Ristorante il Caminetto picks you up in Varenna, zips you up the mountain to his restaurant (experience Italian driving!), and then teaches you some basics of Italian cooking. Learn how to handcraft fresh pasta or prep regional specialties. Classes last about three hours, plus time to *mangiare* (€65 includes trip, lesson, recipes, and lunch complete with wine, cookies, and coffee; Mon, Tue, Thu, and Fri; 10:00 pickup from Varenna landing, return by 16:00, reservations required, tel. 0341-815-127, www.ilcaminettoonline.com, info@ilcaminettoonline.com).

Sleeping in Varenna

Reservations are tight in August, snug May through October, and wide open most of the rest of the year. Many places close in winter. High-season prices are listed here; prices get soft off-season.

$$$$ Hotel du Lac, filling a refined and modernized 19th-century villa, is the finest hotel in town. From its exclusive private perch on the point, it offers a quiet lakefront breakfast terrace; genteel public spaces; a friendly, professional staff; and 16 delightful rooms—all but three with lake views (air-con, some rooms with elevator access, pay parking, Via del Prestino 11, tel. 0341-830-238, www.albergodulac.com, info@albergodulac.com, Valleria).

$$$$ Villa Cipressi is a sprawling, centuries-old lakeside mansion with 33 basic but modern rooms. Its elegant but understated public spaces are often busy with wedding parties. Rooms without views face the street and can be noisy. The villa sits in a huge, quiet, terraced garden that nonguests pay to see (RS%, some view rooms, ceiling fans, elevator, Via IV Novembre 22, tel. 0341-830-113, www.hotelvillacipressi.it, info@hotelvillacipressi.it, Davide).

$$$$ Hotel Royal Victoria, a central splurge facing the main square, has a classic, grand-hotel lobby, an inviting terrace with a swimming pool just above the lake, and 43 richly furnished rooms with modern amenities (RS%, some lake view rooms, air-con, elevator, pay Wi-Fi, pay parking, Piazza San Giorgio 2, tel. 0341-815-111, www.royalvictoria.com, info@royalvictoria.com).

$$$ **Albergo Milano,** right in the old town, is graciously run by Egidio and his Swiss wife, Bettina. Fusing the best of Italy with the best of Switzerland, this well-run, romantic hotel has eight comfortable rooms with extravagant views, balconies, or big terraces (ceiling fans, no elevator; from the station, take main road to town and turn right at steep alley where sidewalk and guardrail break; Via XX Settembre 35, tel. 0341-830-298, www.varenna. net, hotelmilano@varenna.net). This place whispers *luna di miele*— honeymoon (see website for honeymoon deal). Nearby is $$$ **Casa Rossa,** an annex with five comfortable rooms and one apartment that works well for families (breakfast served at main hotel, non-view rooms are more budget-friendly). Their recommended Ristorante la Vista is worth considering for dinner.

$$$ **Hotel Eremo Gaudio** stands out with a commanding lake view high above Varenna. Once an orphanage, it became a hermitage run by the Catholic Church, and then—since 2000—a peaceful hotel with awe-inspiring view balconies and a breakfast terrace. Thirteen bright, plain-but-comfy rooms climb up the main building, and 14 less dramatic but equally comfortable rooms huddle below at the foot of the funicular (all rooms have lake views, air-con in summer; from the station, it's a steep walk up hills and steps—taking a taxi is recommended; 8-minute walk from Varenna's main square at Via Roma 25, tel. 0341-815-301, www. hoteleremovarenna.it, info@hoteleremovarenna.it).

$$$ **Albergo del Sole** rents eight simple, comfortable rooms (with partial-lake or piazza views) above a restaurant right on the town square, which can be lively at night. Run by fun-loving Enzo and Francesco (family rooms, open all year, fans, hardwood floors, shiny bathrooms, elevator, Piazza San Giorgio 17, tel. 0341-815-218, www.albergodelsolevarenna.it, albergo.sole@virgilio.it).

$$ **Hotel Montecodeno,** with 11 decent rooms and no views, is a functional concrete box along the main road. It's a five-minute walk from the train station and ferries (RS%, air-con, no elevator, attached restaurant, Via della Croce 2, tel. 0341-830-123, mobile 340-356-7688, www.hotelmontecodeno.com, info@hotelmontecodeno.com, Marco).

$ **Albergo Beretta,** on the main road a block below the station, has 10 small, basic rooms, several with balconies (and street noise). Second-floor rooms are quietest. Above a coffee shop that doubles as the reception, it feels dated and lacks lakeside glamour, but is a decent budget option (elevator, Wi-Fi in common areas, limited free parking—reserve ahead, Via per Esino 1, tel. 0341-830-132, hotelberetta@iol.it, Renato).

Eating in Varenna

Lavarello, a lake whitefish, is popular on menus. For something more adventurous, consider *missoltino,* which are salted little fish often served with pasta or local-style polenta (buckwheat is mixed in with the corn). *Pizzocchere* is a regional pasta dish made with buckwheat noodles, boiled potatoes, greens, and lots of melty cheese—a carb lover's dream. As with Varenna's hotels, many of these restaurants close off-season (generally November through February or March).

DINING WITH A LAKE VIEW

$$$$ Ristorante la Vista, at Albergo Milano, feels like a private hotel restaurant but also welcomes nonguests. On a balmy evening, their terrace overlooking the town and the lake is hard to beat. Egidio (or Egi—pronounced "edgy") and his staff give traditional cuisine a creative twist, and his selection is great for foodies with discerning tastes. While you can order à la carte, I'd go with his €40 three-course fixed-price dinner (Mon and Wed-Sun 19:00-22:00, closed Sun Oct-mid-May, closed Tue year-round; reservations required, Via XX Settembre 35, tel. 0341-830-298, www.varenna.net).

$$$$ Ristorante la Contrada, with its terrace-side location, is run by the Villa Cipressi and takes advantage of the villa's elegant garden, trickling fountain, and lake view. Indoor seating glows with a warm and romantic air, and the garden is a delight on warm summer evenings. Fresh daily specialties and professional service make this a worthwhile splurge, but weddings can crowd the place and distract from the service (daily 12:15-14:30 & 19:15-22:00, may close Tue, may close for weddings, Via IV Novembre 22, tel. 0341-830-113, www.hotelvillacipressi.it).

DINING WITHOUT A LAKE VIEW

$$$ Ristorante il Cavatappi, a classy little place on a quiet lane just off the town square, has only seven tables, so the cook-and-waiter team can connect personally with diners (Thu-Sun 12:00-14:00 & 18:30-21:00, Mon-Wed 18:30-21:00 only, closed Oct-March, reservations recommended for dinner, Via XX Settembre 10, tel. 0341-815-349, www.cavatappivarenna.it).

$$$ Osteria Quatro Pass is a welcoming bistro known for its homemade pasta, lake fish, and meat. It offers 18 candlelit tables under picturesque vaults, plus sidewalk seating. Its fun energy lets you know that it's a popular spot (daily 12:00-14:00 & 18:30-22:00, closed Mon-Wed in winter, Via XX Settembre 20, tel. 0341-815-091, www.quattropass.com/en; Lilly serves while her son Giuseppe cooks).

$$$ **Varenna Monamour**'s split-level interior, done up with stone and beams, feels sleek but casual. Their menu has a nouvelle-cuisine flair, and they pride themselves on specializing in sea-food—not lake fish (May-Sept daily 12:00-14:30 & 18:30-23:30, shorter hours and closed Tue off-season, Contrada Scoscesa 7, tel. 0341-814-016, www.varennamonamour.it).

EATING SIMPLY ON THE WATER

Along the waterfront in Varenna's old section are two simple eateries, both with great lakefront seating and relaxed (read: slow) service. Either of these is ideal for lingering over affordable (but forgettable) food in a stunning setting.

$$ **Nilus Bar,** with a young waitstaff, serves crêpes, pizzas, big mixed salads, hot sandwiches, soup of the day, a few pastas, and cocktails (daily 12:00-22:30, closed Tue off-season, bar open longer, tel. 0341-815-228, Fulvia and Giovanni).

$$ **Bar Il Molo,** next door, is good for a casual meal on the harbor or a drink with a view (daily 11:00-24:00, tel. 0341-830-070). They also have a room full of gifty edibles for sale.

EATING SIMPLY WITHOUT A LAKE VIEW

$$ **Ristorante del Sole,** facing the town square, serves respectable, well-priced meals and Neapolitan-style pizzas. This family-friendly restaurant provides a fun atmosphere, a cozy, walled-in garden in back, and tables on the square. Try their delicious and hearty *pizzocchere,* a handmade buckwheat pasta with melted cheese, potatoes, and greens (daily 11:00-16:00 & 18:30-late, closed Tue Nov-Feb, free Wi-Fi, Piazza San Giorgio 17, tel. 0341-815-218, www.albergodelsolevarenna.it; Francesco and Enzo).

High Above Town: $$$ Ristorante il Caminetto is a homey, backwoods mountain trattoria in Gittana, a tiny town in the hills above Varenna. Getting there entails a curvy 10-minute drive—they'll pick you up for free in Piazza San Giorgio, deliver you to the restaurant, and then dish up classic fare at small-town prices. Moreno, Rossella, and daughter Francesca take pride in their specialties, including grilled meats and risotto with porcini mushrooms and berries. This is a good place to set a price and trust your host to bring whatever's best (€30 three-course fixed-price meal, open Thu-Tue 19:30-21:30, Sat-Sun also 12:30-14:30, closed Wed, reservations mandatory to confirm pickup from Varenna, Viale Progresso 4, tel. 0341-815-127, mobile 347-331-2238, www.ilcaminettoonline.com).

OTHER EATERIES

$$ Pub l'Orso is the hot spot in town for wine or beer and a light meal. Oozing character, it's behind Hotel Olivedo in a renovated shed that used to be a joiner's workshop (closed Mon). The venerable **$$$ Vecchia Varenna** is the only classy restaurant actually on the harbor (closed Mon). And at **$$$ Hotel Olivedo,** a grand old hotel facing the ferry dock, you can eat in a classic dining hall.

Pizza: The recommended **Nilus Bar** and **Ristorante del Sole** both serve quality, well-priced pizza (see listings earlier). While slightly higher-priced, **Victoria Grill** (at the recommended Hotel Royal Victoria) offers pizza that you can enjoy on-site or as take-away.

Gelato: At **Gelateria Riva,** overlooking the water, get a cup or cone to go, then grab a pillowy seat on the bulkhead. Duilio prepares his gelato fresh every day (ask the day before if you want to watch it being made). Try his *nocciola* (hazelnut) before making your choice (daily 11:00-19:00, open later June-Sept).

A few doors down, Giulia at **La Passerella** makes tasty gelato, as well as refreshing fruit sorbets. Also on the menu are an enticing array of pastries and sweets (daily 10:30-20:30, longer hours in summer).

Picnics: Varenna's two little grocery stores have all you need for a tasty balcony or breakwater picnic. The *salumeria* on the main square is best for meats, cheese, and bread; try their homemade salami (Tue-Sat 8:30-12:30 & 16:00-19:30, Sun-Mon 8:30-12:30 only, Via IV Novembre 2). The **grocery store** just north of the main square by the pharmacy stocks fresh fruits, veggies, and a few essentials (Tue-Sat 8:30-19:00, Sun-Mon until 12:30; Oct-May daily 7:30-12:30 plus Tue-Sat 16:00-19:00, Via Venini 6).

At the Train Station: $ Café III Binario adds charm and class, offering fresh salads, homemade pizza, sandwiches, pasta, pastries, and even breakfast for those with early departures. Enjoy your food on their terrace or take it to go (daily 6:00-21:00, closes earlier off-season).

Varenna Connections

BY TRAIN

Before leaving Varenna, buy your tickets from the I Viaggi del Tivano travel agency in the station. (Or, to avoid lines and stress at the station, buy tickets in advance in the town center at the Barilott bar/tobacco shop just off the main square.) Stamp your ticket in the yellow machine at the station before boarding. If the office is closed and you can't buy tickets, win the sympathy of the conductor and buy your ticket as soon as you get on board for a small additional fee. (Find him before he finds you—or you'll face a €50 fine.)

LAKES

Varenna to Milan: Trains from Varenna to Milano Centrale take about an hour and leave at :37 past most hours (with a few two-hour gaps; confirm schedule at the station or online at www. trenitalia.com). Additional connections require a change in Lecco and an extra 30 minutes.

Varenna to Stresa (on Lake Maggiore): You'll have to take the train back to Milano Centrale, then connect from there to Stresa (3-4 hours).

Varenna to St. Moritz (Switzerland): Take the train from Varenna to Tirano (1.5 hours), where you'll have a layover before boarding the scenic Bernina Express train to St. Moritz (another 2.5 hours, 3 connections/day in summer, 1/day late Oct-early May, www.rhb.ch). A quicker, more frequent, but less scenic route is to take the train to Chiavenna (changing in Colico), then transfer to the bus, which takes you over the Maloja Pass to St. Moritz (5-6/day, 3.5 hours total). For times and tickets, stop by the I Viaggi del Tivano travel agency (see "Helpful Hints," earlier). Don't forget your passport for trips into Switzerland. For more about St. Moritz and scenic trains, consider picking up my guidebook *Rick Steves Switzerland*.

Bellagio

The self-proclaimed "Pearl of the Lake" is a classy combination of tidiness and Old World elegance. If you don't mind that "tramp in a palace" feeling, it's a fine place to shop for ties and umbrellas while surrounding yourself with the more adventurous posh travelers. Heavy curtains between the harborfront arcades create welcome shade and keep visitors and their poodles from sweating. Thriving yet still cute, Bellagio is a much more substantial  town than Varenna. And as much as I'd like to disdain a town that gave its name to a Las Vegas casino, I gotta admit—Bellagio is pretty nice.

Orientation to Bellagio

TOURIST INFORMATION

The TI is at the passenger boat and hydrofoil dock (Mon-Sat 9:00-13:00 & 14:00-18:00, Sun 10:30-12:30 & 13:30-17:30, shorter hours Nov-March, tel. 031-950-204, www.bellagiolakecomo. com). The TI has free brochures for several well-crafted city walking tours, varying from one to three hours. They also sell a hiking map that shows hikes with a range of difficulty and duration.

ARRIVAL IN BELLAGIO

Bellagio is best reached by boat from Varenna or Como.

By Boat: Bellagio has two sets of docks a couple hundred yards apart. (When you depart, be sure you're at the right dock—ask when you buy your ticket.)

By Car: Parking is difficult and the center of town is a no-traffic "ZTL" zone 10:00-18:30—pay attention to signed restrictions. You can try for a spot in the *parco comunale* (west side of town) near the lake, or in the parking lot at the ferry dock. Spaces marked with white lines are always free, yellow lines are for residents only, and blue lines are pay-to-park (use pay-and-display machines—€1.50/hour from 8:00-23:00, free overnight).

HELPFUL HINTS

Market: There's a lakeside market every third Wednesday of the month.

Laundry: La Lavandera is handy. Don't be discouraged if it looks closed; the lights come on automatically when you enter (coins only, change machine, daily 24 hours, Salita Carlo Grandi 21, tel. 339-410-6852).

Sights and Activities in Bellagio

Villa Serbelloni Park

If you need a destination, you can visit this park (accessible only with guided tour), which overlooks the town. The villa itself, owned by the Rockefeller Foundation, is not open to the public.

Cost and Hours: €9, required tour Tue-Sun at 11:00 and 15:30; no tours Mon, Nov-mid-March, or when rainy; 1.5 hours, first two-thirds of walk is uphill, show up at the little tour office in the medieval tower on Piazza della Chiesa 15 minutes before tour time to buy tickets, confirm time at office, tel. 031-951-555.

Strolling

Explore the steep-stepped lanes rising from the harbor-front. While Johnnie Walker and jewelry sell best at lake level, the natives shop up the hill. Piazza della Chiesa, near the top of town, has a worth-a-look church (with a golden

LAKES

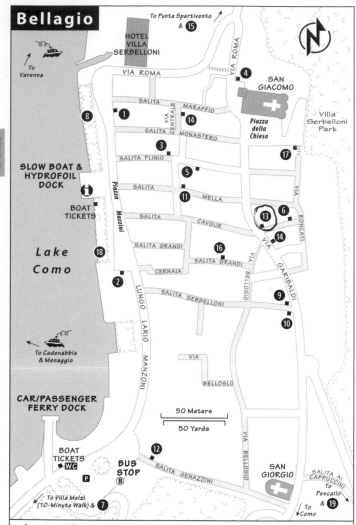

Bellagio

Accommodations
1 Hotel Florence
2 Hotel/Rist./Snack Bar Metropole
3 Hotel Centrale
4 Albergo Europa
5 Il Borgo Apartments
6 Bellagio B&B Apartments
7 To Giardini di Villa Melzini Apartments

Eateries & Other
8 The Florence Ristorante
9 Trattoria San Giacomo
10 Bilacus Ristorante & Aperitivo Et Al
11 Rist. Terrazza Barchetta
12 Enoteca Cava Turacciolo
13 Gelateria del Borgo
14 Groceries (2)
15 To La Punta Ristorante
16 Launderette
17 Villa Serbelloni Park Tickets
18 Bellagio Water Limousines
19 To Bellagio Water Sports

altarpiece under glittering mosaics; pick up the English handout that describes its art).

North of Town: The de facto capital of the mid-lake region, Bellagio is located where the two legs of the lake split off to the south. For an easy break in a park with a great view, wander right on out to the crotch. Meander behind the rich-and-famous Hotel Villa Serbelloni, and walk 10 minutes up a concrete alley to **Punta Spartivento** ("Point that Divides the Wind"). You'll pop out to find a Renoir atmosphere complete with an inviting bar-restaurant (see "Eating in Bellagio," later), a tiny harbor, and a chance to sit on a park bench and gaze north past Menaggio, Varenna, and the end of the lake to the Swiss Alps.

South of Town: For another stroll, head south from the car-ferry dock down the tree-shaded promenade. Ten minutes later, you'll pass the town's concrete swimming area and reach the pleasant **Villa Melzi Gardens.** This lakeside expanse of exotic plants, flowers, trees, and Neoclassical sculpture was assembled by the vice president of Napoleon's Italian Republic in the early 19th century. Although not as elaborate as some of the lake's finer gardens, it has a pleasant, tree-shaded promenade for a lakefront stroll. Gaze across the lake at the Villa Carlotta (straight over, surrounded by greenery—described later, under "More Sights on Lake Como") and imagine the time when aristocrats tried to outdo each other (and showcase their wealth) by creating unique and immense horticulture collections. At the entrance, pick up the map identifying both sculptures and plants (€6.50, daily 9:30-18:30, closed Nov-March, www.giardinidivillamelzi.it). About 15 minutes beyond the far end of the garden, you'll reach San Giovanni, with a pebbly public beach (no showers).

Boating and Water Sports

With a small stand at the boat docks, **Bellagio Water Limousines** (run by Australian Jennine and Italian Luca) offers tours and private service in their luxurious and powerful boat. Their basic 2.5-hour tour, guided by Luca, includes a fun hour at mid-lake, with a float-by of Richard Branson's villa, as well as a stop at Villa del Balbianello, where you'll take an English tour (€55, 10 percent discount if you reserve directly and show this book, price includes entry and tour of villa, generally runs April-Oct Tue and Thu-Sun at 13:30 and also often at 11:00, different tours Mon and Wed, check blackboard for day's offerings or call mobile 338-524-4914, www.bellagiowaterlimousines.com, bellagiowaterlimousines@gmail.com).

At **Bellagio Water Sports,** friendly Michele offers kayaking tours within a 10-minute walk of the town center. His popular two-hour tour (€35) covers the Bellagio coast, while his three-hour tour

(€45) includes a stop at Villa Melzi. He also rents kayaks for those wanting to go solo. Book in advance or call ahead to be sure he is there (no tours Sun, weather-dependent late March and Oct, closed Nov-mid-March, located on Pescallo Bay near Hotel La Pergola at Via Sfondrati 1, mobile 340-394-9375, www.bellagiowatersports. com, info@bellagiowatersports.com).

Sleeping in Bellagio

This is a "boom or bust" lake resort, with high-season prices straight through from May to September, plus a brief shoulder season (with discounted prices) in April and from October to November. Bellagio closes down almost completely from December to February and is only half-open in March.

$$$$ Hotel Florence has a prime lakefront setting in the center of town. The 160-year-old, family-run place features 30 rooms, hardwood floors, bold earth tones with splashes of bright colors, and a rich touch of Old World elegance (some rooms with view and balcony, air-con, elevator, Piazza Mazzini 46, tel. 031-950-342, www.hotelflorencebellagio.it, info@hotelflorencebellagio.it, run by the German Ketzlar family).

$$$ Hotel Metropole, dominating Bellagio's waterfront between the ferry docks, is a grand old place with plush public spaces. Its modern rooms have all the comforts and classic flair. All 42 rooms have lake views, either side or full (air-con, elevator, stunning roof terrace, Piazza Mazzini 1, tel. 031-950-409, www. albergometropole.it, info@albergometropole.it).

$$$ Hotel Centrale, managed with pride and care by Giacomo Borelli, warmly welcomes its guests into a true-blue family operation: Signore Borelli's two sons help out, his mama painted the art, and grandpa crafted much of the Art Deco-era furniture. The 17 bright, comfortable but dated rooms lack views, but the public spaces are generous (air-con, elevator, Salita Plinio 7, tel. 031-951-940, www.hc-bellagio.com, info@hc-bellagio.com).

$$ Albergo Europa, run with low energy, is in a concrete annex behind a restaurant, away from the waterfront. Its nine basic rooms are harmlessly behind the times but get the job done (no elevator, free parking, Via Roma 21, tel. 031-950-471, www. hoteleuropabellagio.it, info@hoteleuropabellagio.it, Marchesi family).

$$ Il Borgo Apartments offers seven efficient, modern units in the old center. Equipped with kitchenettes, these are a great deal for families or small groups. Easygoing Flavio is available for check-in daily 11:00-14:00, or by appointment (RS%, cash preferred, no breakfast, air-con, elevator, Salita Plinio 4, tel. 031-

952-497, mobile 338-193-5559, www.borgoresidence.it, info@borgoresidence.it).

$ Bellagio B&B Apartments rents three units at the top of town, up the street from the *gelateria* (kitchens but no breakfast, Salita Cavour 37, tel. 031-951-680, www.bellagiobedandbreakfast.com, info@bellagiobedandbreakfast.com). Owner Giulio also has five large apartments a 15-minute walk from Bellagio (toward Como, www.bellagioronchi.com).

South of Town: About a 15-minute walk south of Bellagio, **$$ Giardini di Villa Melzi Apartments** features three modern doubles and three studios with kitchenettes in the little harbor of Loppia. A free pass allows guests to take a shortcut to Bellagio through the Villa Melzi Gardens (cash only, no breakfast, free parking, Via Melzi d'Eril 23, at the southern entrance to the gardens, tel. 339-221-4394, www.facebook.com/bellagiowelcome, appbellagio@gmail.com or info@bellagiowelcome.com, Ornella).

Eating in Bellagio

As with Bellagio's hotels, many of these restaurants close off-season (generally December through February or March).

ON THE LAKEFRONT

The restaurants in these two recommended hotels offer wonderful lakeside tables and, considering the setting, acceptable prices.

$$$ The Florence is nicely situated under a trellis of wisteria across from the Hotel Florence, away from the ferry fumes. This is a lovely perch for a drink or dinner (also simpler lunch menu of salads and lighter fare, daily 12:00-14:30 & 19:00-22:00, bar open all day, tel. 031-950-342).

Hotel Metropole's **$$$ Terrazzo Ristorante,** while a mediocre food value, has a full menu and is a relaxing delight with good service. **$$ Hotel Metropole Snack Bar,** next to the restaurant, with good service in a great location, has simple pastas and sandwiches and fine salads (both open long hours daily, restaurant closes for midafternoon break, Piazza Mazzini 1, tel. 031-950-409).

IN THE OLD TOWN, WITHOUT LAKE VIEWS

$$ Trattoria San Giacomo is a high-energy place with traditional cuisine, such as *riso e filetto di pesce* (rice and perch fillet in butter and sage). It has seasonal specials and inviting €25 fixed-price meals (choose meat or fish) based on regional specialties. It offers fun seating on a steep, cobbled lane or tight seating inside (Mon and Wed-Thu 12:00-14:30 & 19:00-21:30, Fri-Sun open later midday and evenings, closed Tue, Salita Serbelloni 45, tel. 031-950-329, www.trattoriabellagio.it, Aurelio).

Across the street and sharing the same owner, **$$ Bilacus Ristorante** has a brighter, more open dining room, a fine garden terrace, an emphasis on wine (including some top-quality vintages by the glass), and a menu with a bit more variety beyond local specials (Tue-Sun 11:30-15:00 & 18:30-22:00, closed Mon, Salita Serbelloni 32, tel. 031-950-480, www.bilacusbellagio.it).

$$$ Ristorante Terrazza Barchetta, set on a terrace with no lake view and bedecked with summery colors, puts a creative twist on regional favorites such as lake fish. Don't confuse it with the street-level bar-trattoria—head up the stairs to the second floor. Reservations are recommended (daily 12:00-14:30 & 19:00-22:15, Salita Mella 13, tel. 031-951-389, www.ristorantebarchetta.com).

OTHER OPTIONS

Wine Tasting: Step into the vaulted stone cellar of the funky **$$ Enoteca Cava Turacciolo** to taste three regional wines with a sampling of cheeses, meats, and breads (€19 for Rick Steves readers, Thu-Tue 10:30-24:00, shorter hours Nov-Dec and March, closed Wed and Jan-Feb, Salita Genazzini 3, tel. 031-950-975, www.cavaturacciolo.it, Norberto and Rosy). **$$ Aperitivo Et Al,** slick and jazzy, is a trendier wine bar; it also offers mixed *salumi* and *formaggi* plates, big fresh salads, and light lunches. There's a great selection of wines by the glass (daily 11:30-24:00, Salita Serbelloni 34, tel. 031-951-523).

Gelato: Residents agree that you won't find the best *gelateria* in town among the sundaes served on the waterfront. Instead, climb to the top of town to **Gelateria del Borgo** (daily 10:00-20:00, longer hours July-Aug, Via Garibaldi 46, tel. 031-950-755, Stefania and Gianfranco).

Picnics: You'll find benches at the park, along the waterfront in town, and lining the promenade south of town. Two little groceries can make sandwiches and also sell a few prepared foods: the fancier **Butti Macelleria e Salumeria,** on the upper street near the *gelateria* (Tue-Sun 8:00-13:00 & 16:00-19:00, closed Mon, Via Garibaldi 42, tel. 031-950-333); and the simpler **Antichi Sapori,** tucked inside the Bistro restaurant, on a cross street below the church (daily 8:30-21:00, Via Centrale 3, tel. 031-950-431).

Punta Spartivento: This dramatic natural park, a 10-minute walk north of town, is a great place for either a picnic or a meal at the family-run **$$ La Punta Ristorante**—try the fish; it was swimming in the lake this morning (daily 11:00-22:00, tel. 031-951-888, www.ristorantelapunta.it).

More Sights on Lake Como

For the best one-day look at Lake Como, take my self-guided ferry tour to get your bearings, and hop off at the towns and villas of your choice. The two main villas worth considering (both described after the tour) are Villa Carlotta—with a sterile, museum-like interior and gorgeous, sprawling gardens—and Villa del Balbianello, a bit harder to reach but with a more striking setting, gardens that are more architectural than botanical, and a fascinating tour of the lived-in interior. If you have time, visit both—they're complementary. In this section, I also describe two other lake towns: Menaggio and Como, plus how to side-trip to Lugano in Switzerland.

LAKES

▲▲Self-Guided Ferry Tour

The best simple day out is to take the *battello navetta* (mid-lake ferry) on its entire 50-minute Varenna-Bellagio-Villa Carlotta-Tremezzo-Lenno route (gener-ally departs Varenna at :23 past each hour, confirm times local-ly). On the return trip, hop off at any sights that interest you: Lenno (to see Villa del Balbi-anello), Villa Carlotta, and/ or Bellagio. This commentary describes what you'll see along

the way, leaving from Varenna, though it's doable from Bellagio too.

Leaving Varenna: Looking back at Varenna from the lake, you'll see Vezio Castle rising above the town, with new Varenna on the left (bigger buildings and modern ferry dock), and old Varenna on the right (tighter, more colorful buildings). The big develop-ment high on the hillside is an ugly example of cronyism (with-out the mayor involved, this would never have happened). Under

the castle is a grove of olives—reputedly the northernmost ones grown in Italy. Because the lake is protected from the north wind, exotic flowers grow well in the lake's many fine gardens. To the right of Varenna's castle are the town cemetery, a lift up to Hotel Eremo Gaudio (a former hermitage), and a spurt of water gushing out of the mountain just above lake level. This is the tiny Fiumelatte, Italy's shortest river.

• *On your way across to Bellagio, take a look around.*

Mid-Lake: The Swiss Alps rise to the north. Directly across the lake from Varenna is Menaggio, and just over the ridge from there are Lugano and the "Swiss Riviera." The winds alternate between north and south. In preindustrial times, traders harnessed the wind to sail up and down the lake. Notice the V-shaped, fjord-like terrain. Lake Como is glacier-cut. And, at more than 1,200 feet deep, it's Europe's deepest lake. You'll cruise past the Punta Spartivento, the bulbous point that literally "splits the wind," and where the two "legs" of the lake join (Lake Lecco is on the left/east, and Lake Como on the right).

• *Before long, you'll be...*

Approaching Bellagio: Survey the park at Punta Spartivento—it's a pleasant walk from town. Bellagio has three times the number of hotel rooms as Varenna, as you can see upon approach. The town, with its strip of swanky hotels, is bookended by Villa Serbelloni (five stars) on the left, dominating the lakefront, and the sprawling Grand Hotel Bretagne (four stars) on the right. In the 19th century, aristocratic Russians hung out in the Serbelloni, and well-heeled English chose the  Bretagne. These days, the Serbelloni is the second-most-luxurious hotel on the lake after Villa d'Este, while Bretagne is mired in a long renovation project.

• *Leaving Bellagio, about half the boats make a stop at **San Giovanni**, a small, nondescript lakefront community just down the shore from Bellagio. Whether your boat stops here or not, soon you'll head across the lake for a stop at...*

Villa Carlotta: Because of lake taxes and high maintenance costs, owners of once-elite villas have been forced to turn them into hotels or to open their doors to the paying public. Since 1927, this has been an example of the latter. One of the finest properties on the lake, Villa Carlotta has some good Neoclassical sculpture (including works by Canova) and one of the lake's lushest gardens (see listing below).

• *The shortest hop on this route (you could walk it in less than 10 minutes) takes you along to the town of...*

Tremezzo: As you leave the dock at Villa Carlotta, notice the Grand Hotel Tremezzo, with its striking Liberty-Style (Art Nouveau) facade and swimming pool floating on the lake. Above the town is a villa built in the 19th-century Romantic Age to resemble a medieval castle (next to the stub of a real one).

After the Tremezzo stop—and just before the Tremezzo church—you'll see a public park with a fountain and balustrade.

When the road separated this land from its villa, its owners gave it to the community. Here the lake is dotted by a string of old villas with elegant landings and gated boathouses. Built in the days before motors, they are now too small for most modern lake boats.

Lenno: This pleasant resort town—with a long, arcing bay sheltering lots of little docks, and a generously shaded promenade—is the boat's last stop.

It's decision time: To see the recommended **Villa del Balbianello,** hop off here. Return boats depart hourly; check the schedule before you set off. If you'd prefer to sail back to **Villa Carlotta, Bellagio,** or **Varenna,** you can probably stay put—this is the end of the line, so the boat's going to turn around and head back that way (but for some departures, you may be evicted and need to wait for the next boat).

▲Villa Carlotta

For gardens and flowers (its forte), this is the best of Lake Como's famed villas—especially in spring, when the many flowers are in bloom. For gardeners, it's worth ▲▲▲. I see the lakes as a break from Italy's art, but if you need a culture fix, Villa Carlotta also offers an elegant Neoclassical interior with a sculpture gallery, including works by Antonio Canova.

Cost and Hours: €10 includes villa/museum and gardens, daily 9:00-19:30, last ticket sold at 18:00, museum closes at 18:30, shorter hours last 2 weeks of March and Oct, open some weekends in Nov-Dec, closed mid-Dec-mid-March, tel. 034-440-405, www.villacarlotta.it.

Getting There: Villa Carlotta, at the southern end of the town of Tremezzo, has its own ferry dock (served by the *battello* passenger ferries). It's also less than a 10-minute walk from the Tremezzo and Cadenabbia docks (each served by a variety of boats). In a pinch, you can also use bus #C10 to zip along the lakefront to Lenno, near Villa del Balbianello (1-2/hour, buy ticket on bus, bus stop to the right as you exit Villa Carlotta).

Visiting the Villa: When buying your ticket, pick up the map that identifies the rooms in the house and the major plant groups in the gardens.

From the entrance, hike up the grand staircase and enter the **villa** itself. The main floor is filled with Neoclassical sculpture, including Antonio Canova's *Maddalena Penitente* and *Palamede* and works by his students (look for the impressive replica of Canova's famous *Love and Psyche Reclining*). There are also pieces by the great Danish sculptor Bertel Thorvaldsen. On the next floor up are generally well-presented special exhibits, and on the top floor are painstakingly appointed period rooms with elegant Empire Style (early-19th-century French) furniture.

Then explore the main attraction, the **gardens,** which sprawl in both directions from the villa. To the south (toward Tremezzo) is the classical Old Garden. To the north, things get more interesting: pretty camellias, luscious azaleas, a maze of rhododendrons, a bamboo garden, and the gasp-worthy Valley of the Ferns—a lush jungle gorge with a river coursing through it.

▲▲Villa del Balbianello

The dreamiest villa on the lake perches on a romantic promontory near Lenno, overlooking Lake Como and facing Bellagio. Built at the end of the 18th century on the remains of an old Franciscan church, today the villa reflects the exotic vision of its last owner, explorer and mountaineer Guido Monzino, who died in 1988—leaving his villa and everything in it to the state. It's well worth paying extra to tour the interior to get to know Monzino, who led  the first Italian expedition to climb Mount Everest in 1973. But the real masterpiece here is the terraced garden and elegant loggia, where the land fits the architecture and landscaping in a lovely way. This is a favorite choice for movie directors when they need a far-out villa to feature; this is where James Bond recovered from a particularly bruising experience in *Casino Royale,* and where Anakin first kissed Padmé (and later married her) in *Star Wars: Episode II—Attack of the Clones.*

Cost and Hours: Garden only-€10, garden with villa tour-€20, Thu-Sun and Tue 10:00-18:00, closed Mon and Wed and mid-Nov-mid-March, last entry to garden 45 minutes before closing, tel. 034-456-110, www.visitfai.it/villadelbalbianello.

Tours: The only way inside the villa is with an English tour. Limited to 15 people per tour, these depart at least hourly (more frequently with demand); the first tour is usually at 11:15 and the last at 16:30.

Getting There: It's at the end of a hilly point next to the town of Lenno. From the Lenno ferry dock, turn left and stroll around to the far end of the harbor (about 5 minutes). Here, you can either pay for a **speedboat shuttle** (€5 one-way, €7 round-trip, 2/hour, mobile 333-410-3854, www.taxiboat.net) or carry on by foot. If you choose to **walk,** continue past the boat dock and through the gate marked *Villa Balbianello,* where two options are clearly sign-posted in kilometers: a 20-minute, 1-kilometer (half-mile) hike (including some up and down), or a more challenging 45-minute, 2.5-kilometer (about 1 mile) huff over the top.

Visiting the Villa: Your visit includes two parts: the villa and the gardens. If walking from the boat and back (taking the shorter 20-minute path), allow a leisurely three hours total for the walk and garden/villa visit.

Poke around the **gardens** while waiting for your villa tour to begin. On the Bellagio-facing side, you'll find a tranquil terrace with sweeping lake views.

Along the path, notice the circular stone shed. Originally used for refrigeration (they used ice from the mountains to keep things cool), today this shed houses the tomb of Guido Monzino. On the opposite side of the point, you'll find a terrace in front of the original Franciscan church (now a gift shop selling overpriced drinks). A WC is nearby, and just down the steps is the dock for the speed-boat return to Lenno.

The 50-minute tour of the **villa** is as fascinating as its larger-than-life former owner. You'll tour the loggia (with a library and a study), then spend the rest of the time seeing 18 of the main building's 25 rooms. While finely decorated, these feel cozy, lived-in, and not too extravagant. Each one gives you a bit more insight into Monzino, from his personal living quarters, to his extensive collection of prehistoric artifacts from around the world, to the top-floor museum of his expeditions, with memorabilia from his North Pole and Mount Everest adventures. You'll see secret passages, learn why his furniture came with handles, and find out what's hiding behind the faux bookcase.

Menaggio

Menaggio—the third of the "big three" mid-lake towns (along with Varenna and Bellagio)—has more urban bulk than its neighbors, but visitors are charmed by its lovely lakefront park. Since many find Lake Como too dirty for swimming, consider spending time in Menaggio's fine public pool (look for the *lido*). This is the starting point for a few hikes. (Just a few decades ago, ciga-

rette smugglers used these trails at night to sneak back into Italy from Switzerland with their tax-free booty.) The TI has information about mountain biking and catching the bus to trailheads on nearby Mount Grona. Ask for the free *Walking in the Province of Como* booklet, with information on 18 different walks detailing historical, artistic, and natural features (**TI** on Piazza Garibaldi, tel. 0344-32-924, www.menaggio.com, infomenaggio@tiscali.it).

Sleeping in Menaggio: ¢ La Primula Youth Hostel is a classic, old-school hostel, offering sailing lessons, Italian-language courses, cooking classes, kayak and bike rentals, and a great location on the lake, a two-minute walk from the ferry dock (Via IV Novembre 106, tel. 0344-32356, www.lakecomohostel.com, info@lakecomohostel.com).

Menaggio Connections: In addition to being connected to Varenna and Bellagio by all the regular boats, bus #C10 connects Menaggio to **Como town** in about an hour (1-2/hour). Menaggio is also a springboard for visiting Switzerland. Public bus #C12 departs about every hour or two from Piazza Roma for **Lugano** (around €10 round-trip, 1 hour, buy tickets at bus stop on Via Calvi). In summer, the yellow Palm Express bus runs once daily to **St. Moritz** (3.5 hours; off-season runs only weekends; reservations are required, www.postbus.ch)—remember to bring your passport.

Como Town

On the southwest tip of the lake, Como has a good, traffic-free old town, an interesting Gothic/Renaissance cathedral, a cable car up to a mountaintop viewpoint, and a pleasant lakefront with a promenade (**TI** at Piazza Cavour 17, tel. 031-269-712, www.lakecomo.it). It's an easy 10-minute walk from the boat dock to the train station (trains to Milan depart about twice per hour, 30-60 minutes).

All-Day Lugano Side-Trip

From Varenna or Bellagio, you can make a loop that lets you nip into Switzerland to see the elegant lake resort of Lugano, pass through the town of Como, and cruise a good part of Lake Como. Here's a good day plan (times are approximate—confirm schedules locally): about 9:30—ferry to Menaggio (15 minutes from Varenna); 10:30—bus to Lugano (1 hour, bring your passport); 11:30—explore Lugano; 16:00—train to Como (45 minutes); 17:00/18:00/19:00—fast hydrofoil from Como to Varenna (1 hour). For more information on Lugano, see www.ricksteves.com/lugano.

Lake Maggiore

Lake Maggiore is ringed by mountains, snowcapped in spring and fall, and lined with resort towns such as Stresa. Although Lake  Maggiore lacks the cozy charm of Lake Como, a visit here may be worth the trouble for two islands, both with exotic gardens and lovely villas built by the Borromeo family.

The Borromeos—through many generations since 1630—lovingly turned their islands into magical retreats, with elaborate villas and fragrant gardens. Isola Bella has a palace and terraced garden; Isola Madre has a villa and sprawling English-style (more casual) garden. A third island, Isola Superiore (a.k.a. Isola Pescatori), is simply small, serene, and residential. The Borromeos, who made their money from trade and banking, enjoyed the arts—from paintings (hung in lavish abundance throughout the palace and villa) to plays (performed in an open-air theater on Isola Bella) and marionette shows (you'll see the puppets that once performed here). Although it's a characterless resort, the town of Stresa is a handy departure point for exploring Lake Maggiore's exotic garden islands.

Tourists flock here in May and June, when flowers are in bloom, and in September. Concerts held in scenic settings draw music lovers, particularly during the summer Stresa Festival (get details from Stresa TI). For fewer crowds, visit in April, July, August (when Italians prefer the Mediterranean beaches), or October. In winter, the snow-covered mountains (with resorts a 1.5-hour drive away) attract skiers.

PLANNING YOUR TIME

This region is best visited on a sunny day, when the mountains are clear, the lake is calm, and the heat of the sun brings out the scent of the blossoms. The two top islands for sightseeing are Isola Bella and Isola Madre (if tight on time, focus on Isola Bella). Isola Superiore has no sights, but is a peaceful place for lunch. You can stay the night in Stresa, but a day trip is sufficient for most.

Day Trip from Milan: Catch the one-hour, early train from Milan to the town of Stresa (usually at 8:25, which may require reservations, and likely also at 9:29—but check times carefully, as there's often a midmorning gap until 11:25). Upon arrival in Stresa, walk 10 minutes downhill to the boat dock, and catch a boat to Isola Madre. Work your way back to Isola Superiore for a lazy lunch, and then go on to Isola Bella for the afternoon, before returning to Stresa and back to Milan (trains leave about hourly—jot down your departure options on arrival in Stresa).

GETTING AROUND LAKE MAGGIORE

Boats link the islands and Stresa, running about twice hourly. Allow roughly 10 minutes between stops. Short round-trip hops can add up fast (€6.80 for Isola Bella, €7.80 for Isola Superiore, €10 for Isola Madre, €12.40 for Villa Taranto), so it's usually best to buy a **free circulation ticket,** which allows you to get off and on at intermediate stops between your departure and arrival ports (€13.80 includes Bella and Superiore, €16.90 covers all the islands, and €20.70 includes the islands and Villa Taranto).

Boats run daily April through September. The route: Stresa, Carciano/Lido (at the base of the cable car—but most boats skip this stop), Isola Bella, Isola Superiore, Baveno (lakeside town), Isola Madre, Pallanza, and Villa Taranto. This route is part of a longer one. To follow the boat schedule (free, available at boat docks and the TI), look at the Arona-Locarno timetable for trips from Stresa to the islands, and the Locarno-Arona timetable for the return trip to Stresa. Off-season, the boats cover a shorter route (public boat info: toll-free tel. 800-551-801, www.navigazionelaghi.it).

Buy boat tickets directly from the dock ticket booth under the gallery to the left of the TI. On the promenade to the boat dock, don't be fooled by the private taxi-boat drivers, most dressed in sailor outfits—they'll try to talk you into paying way too much for private tours on their smaller boats.

Sights on Lake Maggiore

Don't linger in Stresa—it's just a functional springboard. The main attractions are the islands and gardens.

STRESA

The town of Stresa—which means "thin stretch"—was named for the original strip of fishermen's huts that lined the shore. Today, grand old hotels run along that same shore.

Arrival in Stresa: At the train station, ask for a free city map at the newsstand (to the far right of the tracks as you exit the train). To get downtown, exit right from the station and take your first left (on Viale Duchessa di Genova). This takes you straight down to the lake (once you're there, the boat dock is about four blocks to your right; ask for boat schedule at ticket window). The helpful **TI** is located to the right of the ticket window at the boat dock (daily 10:00-12:30 & 15:00-18:30, off-season closed Sat afternoon and all day Sun, Piazza Marconi 16, tel. 0323-31308, www.stresaturismo.

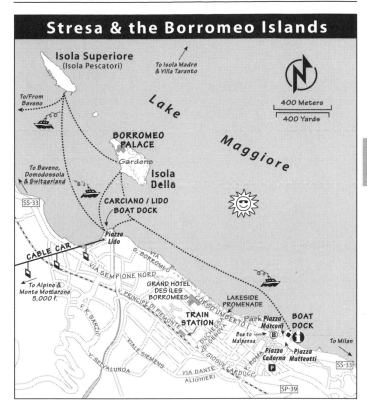

Stresa & the Borromeo Islands

Isola Superiore (Isola Pescatori)

To Isola Madre & Villa Taranto

400 Meters
400 Yards

To/From Baveno

Lake

Maggiore

LAKES

BORROMEO PALACE

Gardens

Isola Bella

To Baveno, Domodossola & Switzerland

SS-33

CARCIANO / LIDO BOAT DOCK

Piazza Lido

CABLE CAR

To Alpino & Monte Mottarone 5,000 f.

VIA SEMPIONE NORD

VIA G. BORROMEO

CORSO UMBERTO

V. PRINCIPE DI PIEMONTE

V. F. SANZIO

VIALE SIEMENS

V. SELVALUNGA

V. DUCHESSA DI GENOVA

V. GIOSUE CARDUCCI

V. ROMA

VIA DANTE ALIGHIERI

GRAND HOTEL DES ILES BORROMEES

TRAIN STATION

Park

Piazza Marconi

LAKESIDE PROMENADE

BOAT DOCK

Bus to Malpensa

B

Piazza Cadorna

Piazza Matteotti

P

To Milan

SS-33

SP-39

it). Taxis charge a fixed rate of €11 for even the shortest ride in town.

Visiting Stresa: The **old town**—basically a traffic-free touristy shopping mall—is just a few blocks deep, stretching inland from the main boat dock. Stresa's stately 19th-century lakeside hotels date back to the days when this town was on the Grand Tour circuit.

In any Romantic Age resort like Stresa, hotels had names designed to appeal to Victorian aristocrats...like Regina Palace (rather than Palazzo), Astoria, Bristol, and Victoria.

The **Grand Hotel des Iles Borromees** was the first (built in 1862). In 1918, 19-year-old Ernest Hemingway—wounded in Slovenia as an ambulance driver for the Italian Red Cross—was taken to Stresa's Grand Hotel des Iles Borromees, which served, like its regal neighbors, as an infirmary during World War I. Hemingway returned to the same hotel in 1948, stayed in the same room (#205, now called the "Hemingway suite"—you can stay there for a couple thousand dollars a night), and signed the guest book as "an old client." Another "old client" was Winston Churchill, who honeymooned here.

A fine waterfront promenade leads past the venerable old hotels to the Lido, with the Carciano boat dock and the **Stresa-Alpino-Mottarone cable car.** This cable car takes you up—in two stages and a 20-minute ride—to the top of Mount Mottarone (€19 round-trip to the top, €11.50 one-way, daily 9:30-17:30 in summer, shorter winter hours, 2-3/hour, bar midway up, tel. 0323-30295, www.stresa-mottarone.it). From the top (about 5,000 feet), you get great panoramic views of neighboring peaks and, by taking a short hike, a bird's-eye view of the small, neighboring Lake Orta (described later).

Halfway up the cable-car line are the **Alpine Gardens,** which come with fine lake views and picnic spots, but these gardens can't compare with what you'll see on the islands. To visit the gardens, get off at the midway Alpino stop and walk 10 minutes (turn left as you leave; €4, daily 9:30-18:00, closed Nov-March). If you plan to hike down, pick up the *Trekking* map from the TI and allow four hours from the top of Mount Mottarone, or two hours from the Alpine Gardens (mountain biking also possible—ask at TI).

Sleeping in Stresa: Because Stresa's town generally lacks appeal, I'd day-trip from Milan. But if you'd like to stay, here are some options: **$$$ Hotel Milan Speranza Au Lac** is a big, group-oriented hotel facing the boat dock (www.milanspweranza.it); **$$ Hotel Saini Meublè** is a small, homey, affordable choice in the old town center (www.hotelsaini.it); and **$$ Hotel Moderno** is a midsize, midrange option in the old town (www.hms.it).

Eating in Stresa: The main square, **Piazza Cadorna,** is one big tourist trap, yet it does have a certain charm. (At night, it seems anyone who claims to be a musician can get a gig singing for diners.) For a (slightly) less touristy alternative, seek out one of these options: **$$ Osteria degli Amici,** tucked away under a vine trellis on a forgotten square a couple of blocks beyond Piazza Cadorna (Via Bolongaro 33); **$$ La Botte,** with an old-school diner vibe on the main street between the port and the square (Via Mazzini 6); or **$$$$ Il Clandestino,** a fancier, romantic, modern splurge specializing in fish (Via Rosmini 5).

ISLANDS AND GARDENS
▲▲Isola Bella

This island, nearest Stresa, has a formal garden and a fancy Baroque palace. Looking like a stepped pyramid from the water, the island was named by Charles

Borromeo (sponsor of Milan's Duomo) for his wife, Isabella. The island itself is touristy, with a gauntlet of souvenir stands and a corral of restaurants. A few back streets provide evidence that people actually live here. While the Borromeo family now lives in Milan, they spend a few weeks on Isola Bella each summer (when their blue-and-red family flag flies from the top of the garden).

Cost and Hours: Palace and garden-€15, €20.50 combo-ticket includes villa at Isola Madre, daily 9:00-18:00, shorter hours for palace's picture gallery, closed late-Oct-late-March, tel. 0323-30556, www.isoleborromee.it.

Tours: A fine €3 audioguide describes the palace, which also has posted English descriptions. A €1.50 booklet explains the gardens.

Services: A WC is located halfway through your visit, where you leave the villa and enter the gardens.

Eating: Several restaurants cluster between the boat docks and the villa. Picnicking is not allowed in the garden, but you can picnic in the pebbly park at the point of the island, beyond the villa (free and open to the public).

Visiting the Island: There are two docks on this island, one for each direction. It's a short walk from the boat to the hulking villa (turn left from the dock; on the way, you'll pass a public WC). Once inside, your visit is a one-way tour, starting with the palace and finishing with the garden. (There's no way to see the garden without the palace.)

In the lavishly decorated Baroque **palace,** stairs lead up under stucco crests of Italy's top families (balls signify the Medici, bees mean the Barberini, and a unicorn symbolizes the Borromeos' motto: Humility). You'll loop through the picture gallery, containing 130 beautifully restored 16th-century paintings from the Borromeo family's private collection, hung wall-to-ceiling in several cramped rooms. Then you'll get a peek at the canopied bed chambers and ogle the ornate throne room. Continue through the dining room, with a portrait of the first Borromeo, and into a richly stuccoed grand hall, with an 80-foot-high dome and featuring an 18th-century model of the villa, including a grand water entry that never materialized.

Next comes the music room, the site of the 1935 Stresa Conference, in which Mussolini met with British and French diplomats in a united attempt to scare Germany out of starting World War II. Look for a copy of the treaty with Mussolini's signature on the wall next to the exit. Unfortunately, the "Stresa Front" soon fizzled when Mussolini attacked Ethiopia and joined forces with Hitler.

Napoleon's bedroom comes with an engraving that depicts his 1797 visit (Napoleon is on a bench with his wife and sister enjoying festivities in his honor). Continue through several more opulent halls, many of which display souvenirs and gifts that the Borromeo family picked up over the generations.

Downstairs, many of the famous Borromeo marionettes are on display. (A larger collection is on Isola Madre.) The 18th-century, multiroom grotto, decorated from ceiling to floor with shell motifs and black-and-white stones, still serves its original function of providing a cool refuge from Italy's heat. The dreamy marble statues are by Gaetano Monti, a student of Antonio Canova. Climbing out of the basement, look up at the unique, cantilevered, spiral stairs; they're from a 16th-century fortress that predates this building.

Pass through the mirrored corridor and follow the route through more rooms until you come to the ornate hall of 16th-century Flemish tapestries. This leads to the finale of this island visit: the beautiful **garden,** complete with Chinese white peacocks, which give it an exotic splash. (Before continuing to the garden, consider heading up the stairs near the WC to stroll through Elisa's Greenhouse, named for Napoleon's sister and home to tropical plants.)

From the palace, head straight up the stairs into the main part of the garden. Baroque—which is exactly what you see here—is all about controlling nature. The centerpiece is a pyramid-shaped outdoor grotto, crowned by the Borromeo family unicorn. Up the stairs and behind this fanciful structure is a vast terrace with views over the lower gardens and Stresa. Back downstairs, follow the signs (hidden in the bushes) to the café and bookshop, which anchor the far points of the island, to see the terraces behind the "pyramid." Finally, follow *exit* signs to pop out a side gate at the top of a twisty, stepped lane back through town to the boat docks.

▲Isola Superiore (Pescatori)

This sleepy island—home to 35 families—is the smallest and most residential of the three. It has a few good fish restaurants, ample

pizza-by-the-slice take-out joints, picnic benches, views, and, blissfully, nothing much to do—all under arbors of wisteria. Simply stroll the narrow, cobbled lanes, or relax at the long, skinny, pebbly park/beach at the tip of the island. A delight for photographers and painters, the island is never really crowded, except at lunchtime.

▲Isola Madre

Don't come to this island unless you intend to tour the sight, because that's all there is: an interesting furnished villa and a lovely garden filled with exotic birds and plants.

Cost and Hours: Villa and garden–€12, €20.50 combo-ticket includes Isola Bella, daily 9:00-18:00, closed late-Oct-late-March, tel. 0323-31261, www.isoleborromee.it.

Information: The villa has a few sparse English descriptions. Garden lovers can invest a few euros in a booklet about the plantings.

Services: A WC is next to the chapel. You'll also find a café/bookshop (selling basic sandwiches) just outside the villa. While eating is best on Isola Superiore, Isola Madre has one real restaurant, **La Piratera Ristorante Bar,** which owns a big, beautiful terrace over the lake. You'll run into this immediately after leaving the villa/garden complex (€24 fixed-price tourist meal, daily 8:00-18:00, sit-down meals 12:00-15:30, simple sandwiches and slices of pizza-to-go anytime, picnic at the rocky beach a minute's walk from the restaurant, just to your right as you exit the gardens, tel. 032-331-171).

Visiting the Island: Visiting is a one-way affair. From the boat dock, walk up the stairs to the ticket desk for the villa. Then, once through the gate, take the level path to the right to loop around the gardens and end at the villa (*ingresso al giardino* signs). Or, if you're in a rush, take the stairs to the left instead to go straight to the villa.

First you'll circle all the way around the **gardens.** Eight gardeners (with the help of water continually pumped from the lake) keep this English-style garden paradise lush. It's a joy, even for those bored by flowers and foliage. You'll see trees from around the world, and an exotic bird menagerie with golden and silver pheasants and Chinese peacocks. (You'll see and hear them roaming wild; also look for the bird cages partway up the main staircase to the villa, on the left.)

In front of the villa, a once-magnificent **Himalayan cypress tree** paints your world a streaky green. The 150-year-old tree, knocked down by a tornado in 2006 but successfully saved, is an attraction in its own right, with steel guy-wires now anchoring it firmly in place.

The 16th-century **villa** is the first of the Borromeo palaces. A century older than the Isola Bella villa, it's dark, somber, and dates from the Renaissance. The clever angled hinges keep the doors from flapping in the lake breeze. The family's huge collection of dolls, marionettes, and exquisite 17th-century marionette theater sets—painted by a La Scala opera set designer—fills several rooms. A corner room is painted to take you into an 18th-century Venetian Rococo sitting room under a floral greenhouse.

Some of the garden's best flowers are in view immediately after leaving the villa. Walk down the stairs to the terrace in front of the chapel, with WCs tucked around the left side. Stairs lead directly down to the boat dock from here. Or you can loop past the villa to exit at the far end, just above La Piratera restaurant. From there, you can walk through the shop to reach a terrace path that leads you back to the boat dock.

Villa Taranto Botanical Gardens

Garden lovers will enjoy this large landscaped park, located on the mainland across the lake from Stresa. Although it's the most sprawling garden in the area, and enjoyable for a stroll in a park, it's a bit underwhelming. The gardens are a Scotsman's labor of love. Starting in the 1930s, Neil McEacharn created this garden of delights—bringing in thousands of plants from all over the world—and here he stays, in the small mausoleum. The park's highlight is a terraced garden with a series of cascading pools. Villa Taranto is directly across the street from the boat dock.

Cost and Hours: €10, daily 8:30-18:30, Oct 9:00-16:00, closed Nov-mid-March, tel. 0323-404-555, www.villataranto.it.

Getting There: It's two stops (about 15 minutes) past Isola Madre. On the way, you'll pass a scenic promontory speckled with villas. Note that only about half of the lake boats stop here, which means an hour between return departures—check schedules carefully.

DAY TRIP FROM STRESA

▲Lake Orta

Just on the other side of Mount Mottarone is the small lake of Orta. The lake's main town, Orta San Giulio, has a beautiful lakeside piazza ringed by picturesque buildings. The piazza faces the

lake with a view of Isola San Giulio. Taxi boats (€4 round-trip) make the five-minute trip throughout the day. The island is worth a look for the Church of San Giulio and the circular "path of silence," which takes about 10 minutes. In peak season, Orta is anything but silent, but off-season or early or late in the day, this place is full of peace and magic (TI on Via Panoramica next to the parking lot downhill from the train station, tel. 0322-905-163).

Getting There: The train ride from Stresa to Orta-Miasino (a short walk from the lakeside piazza) takes 1.5-2 hours and requires a change or two (5/day). Public buses from Stresa's Piazza Marconi to Orta depart from near the TI (around €9 round-trip, about 1 hour, 2-3/day mid-June-mid-Sept, confirm schedule at TI or at www.safduemila.com).

LAKES

PRACTICALITIES

This section covers just the basics on traveling in Italy (for much more information, see *Rick Steves Italy*). You'll find free advice on specific topics at www.ricksteves.com/tips.

Money

Italy uses the euro currency: 1 euro (€) = about $1.20. To convert prices in euros to dollars, add about 20 percent: €20 = about $24, €50 = about $60. (Check www.oanda.com for the latest exchange rates.)

The standard way for travelers to get euros is to withdraw money from an ATM (known as a *bancomat*) using a debit or credit card, ideally with a Visa or MasterCard logo. To keep your cash, cards, and valuables safe, wear a money belt.

Before departing, call your bank or credit-card company: Confirm that your card(s) will work overseas, ask about international transaction fees, and alert them that you'll be making withdrawals in Europe. Also ask for the PIN number for your credit card—you may need it for Europe's "chip-and-PIN" payment machines (see below; allow time for your bank to mail your PIN to you).

Dealing with "Chip and PIN": Most credit and debit cards now have chips that authenticate and secure transactions. European cardholders insert their chip card into the payment slot, then enter a PIN. (For most US cards, you provide a signature.) Any American card, whether with a chip or an old-fashioned magnetic stripe, will work at Europe's hotels, restaurants, and shops. But some self-service chip-and-PIN payment machines—such as those at train stations, toll roads, or unattended gas pumps—may not accept your card, even if you know the PIN. If your card won't work, look for a cashier who can process the transaction manually—or pay in cash.

Dynamic Currency Conversion: If merchants or hoteliers offer to convert your purchase price into dollars (called dynamic currency conversion, or DCC), refuse this "service." You'll pay extra in fees for the expensive convenience of seeing your charge in dollars. If an ATM offers to "lock in" or "guarantee" your conversion rate, choose "proceed without conversion." Other prompts might state, "You can be charged in dollars: Press YES for dollars, NO for euros." Always choose the local currency.

Staying Connected

The simplest solution is to bring your own device—mobile phone, tablet, or laptop—and use it just as you would at home (following the tips below, such as connecting to free Wi-Fi whenever possible).

To call Italy from a US or Canadian number: Whether you're phoning from a landline, your own mobile phone, or a Skype account, you're making an international call. Dial 011-39 and then the local number. (The 011 is our international access code, and 39 is Italy's country code.) If dialing from a mobile phone, you can enter + in place of the international access code—press and hold the 0 key.

To call Italy from a European country: Dial 00-39 followed by the local number. (The 00 is Europe's international access code.)

To call within Italy: Just dial the local number.

To call from Italy to another country: Dial 00 followed by the country code (for example, 1 for the US or Canada), then the area code and number. If you're calling European countries whose phone numbers begin with 0, you'll usually omit that 0 when you dial.

Tips: If you bring your own mobile phone, consider getting an international plan; most providers offer a global calling plan that cuts the per-minute cost of phone calls and texts, and a flat-fee data plan.

Use Wi-Fi whenever possible. Most hotels and many cafés offer free Wi-Fi, and you'll likely also find it at tourist information offices, major museums, and public-transit hubs. With Wi-Fi you can use your phone or tablet to make free or inexpensive domestic and international calls via a calling app such as Skype, FaceTime, or Google+ Hangouts. When you can't find Wi-Fi, you can use your cellular network to connect to the Internet, send texts, or make voice calls. When you're done, avoid further charges by manually switching off "data roaming" or "cellular data."

It's possible to stay connected without a mobile device. Most hotels have a computer in the lobby for guests to use. To make cheap international calls from any phone (even your hotel-room phone), you can buy a prepaid international phone card in Italy. Dial the toll-free access number, enter the card's PIN code, then

Sleep Code

Hotels are classified based on the average price of a standard double room with breakfast in high season.

$$$$	**Splurge:** Most rooms over €170
$$$	**Pricier:** €130-170
$$	**Moderate:** €90-130
$	**Budget:** €50-90
¢	**Backpacker:** Under €50
RS%	**Rick Steves discount**

Unless otherwise noted, credit cards are accepted, hotel staff speak basic English, and free Wi-Fi is available. Comparison-shop by checking prices at several hotels (on each hotel's own website, on a booking site, or by email). For the best deal, book directly with the hotel. Ask for a discount if paying in cash; if the listing includes **RS%,** request a Rick Steves discount.

dial the number. For more on phoning, see www.ricksteves.com/phoning. For a one-hour talk on "Traveling with a Mobile Device," see www.ricksteves.com/travel-talks.

Sleeping

I've categorized my recommended accommodations based on price, indicated with a dollar-sign rating (see sidebar). I recommend reserving rooms in advance, particularly during peak season. Once your dates are set, check the specific price for your preferred stay at several hotels. You can do this either by comparing prices on Hotels.com or Booking.com, or by checking the hotels' own websites. To get the best deal, contact my family-run hotels directly by phone or email. When you go direct, the owner avoids the online booking engine commission, giving them wiggle room to offer you a discount, a nicer room, or free breakfast. If you prefer to book online or are considering a hotel chain, it's to your advantage to use the hotel's website.

For complicated requests, send an email with the following information: number and type of rooms; number of nights; arrival date; departure date; and any special requests. Use the European style for writing dates: day/month/year. Hoteliers typically ask for your credit-card number as a deposit.

Some hotels are willing to make a deal to attract guests: Try emailing several to ask their best price. In general, hotel prices can soften if you do any of the following: offer to pay cash, stay at least three nights, or travel off-season.

While most taxes are included in the price, a variable city tax of €1.50-5/person per night is often added to hotel bills in Italy. Some hoteliers will ask to collect the city tax in cash to make their bookkeeping and accounting simpler.

Restaurant Price Code

I've assigned each eatery a price category, based on the average cost of a typical main course (pasta or *secondi*). Drinks, desserts, and splurge items (steak and seafood) can raise the price considerably.

$$$$ **Splurge:** Most main courses over €20
$$$ **Pricier:** €15-20
$$ **Moderate:** €10-15
$ **Budget:** Under €10

In Italy, pizza by the slice and other takeaway food is **$**; a basic trattoria or sit-down pizzeria is **$$**; a casual but more upscale restaurant is **$$$**; and a swanky splurge is **$$$$**.

Eating

I've categorized my recommended eateries based on price, indicated with a dollar-sign rating (see sidebar). Italy offers a wide array of eateries. A *ristorante* is a formal restaurant, while a *trattoria* or *osteria* is usually more traditional and simpler (but can still be pricey). Italian "bars" are not taverns, but small cafés selling sandwiches, coffee, and other drinks. An *enoteca* is a wine bar with snacks and light meals. Take-away food from pizza shops and delis (*rosticcería*) makes an easy picnic.

Italians eat dinner a bit later than we do; better restaurants start serving around 19:00. A full meal consists of an appetizer (antipasto), a first course (*primo piatto*, pasta, rice, or soup), and a second course (*secondo piatto*, expensive meat and fish/seafood dishes). Vegetables *(verdure)* may come with the *secondo*, but more often must be ordered separately as a side dish (*contorno*). Desserts (*dolci*) can be very tempting. The euros can add up in a hurry, but you don't have to order each course. My approach is to mix antipasti and *primi piatti* family-style with my dinner partners (skipping *secondi*). Or, for a basic value, look for a *menù del giorno*, a three- or four-course, fixed-price meal deal (avoid the cheapest ones, often called a *menù turistico*).

At bars and cafés, getting a drink while standing at the bar (*banco*) is cheaper than drinking it at a table *(tavolo)* or sitting outside *(terrazza)*. This tiered pricing system is clearly posted on the wall. Sometimes you'll pay at a cash register, then take the receipt to another counter to claim your drink.

Good service is relaxed (slow to an American). You won't get the bill until you ask for it: *"Il conto?"* Many (but not all) restaurants in Italy add a cover charge *(coperto)* of €1-3.50 per person to your bill.

Tipping: Most restaurants include a service charge in their prices (check the menu for *servizio incluso*—generally around 10 percent). You can add on a tip, if you choose, by including a euro or two for each person in your party. If you order at a counter rather than from waitstaff, there's no need to tip.

Transportation

By Train: In Italy, most travelers find it's cheapest simply to buy train tickets as they go. To see if a rail pass could save you money, check www.ricksteves.com/rail. To research train schedules, visit Germany's excellent all-Europe website, www.bahn.com, or Italy's www.trenitalia.com. A private company called Italo also runs fast trains on major routes in Italy; see www.italotreno.it.

You can buy tickets at train stations (at the ticket window or at machines with English instructions) or from travel agencies. Before boarding the train, you must validate your train documents by stamping them in the machine near the platform (usually marked *convalida biglietti* or *vidimazione*). Strikes *(sciopero)* are common and generally announced in advance (but a few sporadic trains still run—ask around).

By Bus: Long-distance buses are catching on in Italy as an alternative to the train. They are usually cheaper, modern, and often (unlike trains) have free Wi-Fi. Some of the operators you'll see are Eurolines/Baltour (www.baltour.it), Flixbus (www.flixbus.com), and Marozzi (www.marozzivt.it).

By Car: It's cheaper to arrange most car rentals from the US. If you're planning a multicountry itinerary by car, be aware of often-astronomical international drop-off fees. For tips on your insurance options, see www.ricksteves.com/cdw, and for route planning, consult www.viamichelin.com. Theft insurance is mandatory in Italy ($15-20/day). In Italy, most car-rental companies' rates automatically include Collision Damage Waiver (CDW) coverage. Even if you try to decline CDW when you reserve your Italian car, you may find when you show up at the counter that you must buy it after all.

It's also required that you carry an International Driving Permit (IDP), available at your local AAA office ($20 plus two passport-type photos, www.aaa.com).

Italy's superhighway *(autostrada)* system is slick and speedy, but you'll pay a toll. Be warned that car traffic is restricted in many city centers—don't drive or park in any area that has a sign reading *Zona Traffico Limitato* (*ZTL,* often shown above a red circle)...or you might be mailed a ticket later.

Italians love to tailgate; otherwise, local road etiquette is similar to that in the US. Ask your car-rental company for details, or check the US State Department website (www.travel.state.gov, search for Italy in the "Learn about your destination" box, then click on "Travel and Transportation").

A car is a worthless headache in cities—park it safely (get tips from your hotelier). As break-ins are common, be sure your valuables are out of sight and locked in the trunk, or even better, with you or in your hotel room.

Helpful Hints

Emergency Help: For English-speaking **police** help, dial 113. To summon an **ambulance**, call 118. For passport problems, call the **US Embassy** (in Rome, 24-hour line—tel. 06-46741) or **US Consulates** (Milan—tel. 02-290-351, Florence—tel. 055-266-951, Naples—tel. 081-583-8111); or the **Canadian Embassy** (in Rome, tel. 06-854-442-911). If you have a minor illness, do as the locals do and go to a pharmacist for advice. Or ask at your hotel for help—they'll know of the nearest medical and emergency services. For other concerns, get advice from your hotelier.

Theft or Loss: Italy has particularly hardworking pickpockets—wear a money belt. Assume beggars are pickpockets and any scuffle is simply a distraction by a team of thieves. If you stop for any commotion or show, put your hands in your pockets before someone else does.

To replace a passport, you'll need to go in person to an embassy or consulate (see above). Cancel and replace your credit and debit cards by calling these 24-hour US numbers collect: Visa—tel. 303/967-1096, MasterCard—tel. 636/722-7111, American Express—tel. 336/393-1111. In Italy, to make a collect call to the US, dial 800-172-4444; press zero or stay on the line for an operator. File a police report either on the spot or within a day or two; you'll need it to submit an insurance claim for lost or stolen rail passes or travel gear, and it can help with replacing your passport or credit and debit cards. For more information, see www.ricksteves.com/help.

Time: Italy uses the 24-hour clock. It's the same through 12:00 noon, then keep going: 13:00, 14:00, and so on. Italy, like most of continental Europe, is six/nine hours ahead of the East/West Coasts of the US.

Business Hours: Many businesses have now adopted the government's recommended 8:00 to 14:00 workday (although in tourist areas, shops are open longer). Still, expect small towns and villages to be more or less shut tight during lunch. Stores are also usually closed on Sunday, and often on Monday.

Sights: Opening and closing hours of sights can change unexpectedly; confirm the latest times with the local tourist information office or its website. Some major churches enforce a modest dress code (no bare shoulders or shorts) for everyone, even children.

Holidays and Festivals: Italy celebrates many holidays, which can close sights and attract crowds (book hotel rooms ahead). For information on holidays and festivals, check Italy's website: www. italia.it. For a simple list showing major—though not all—events, see www.ricksteves.com/festivals.

Numbers and Stumblers: What Americans call the second floor of a building is the first floor in Europe. Europeans write dates as day/month/year, so Christmas 2019 is 25/12/19. Commas are decimal points and vice versa—a dollar and a half is 1,50, and there are 5.280 feet in a mile. Italy uses the metric system: A kilogram is 2.2 pounds; a liter is about a quart; and a kilometer is six-tenths of a mile.

Resources from Rick Steves

This Snapshot guide is excerpted from my latest edition of *Rick Steves Italy,* one of many titles in my ever-expanding series of guidebooks on European travel. I also produce a public television series, *Rick Steves' Europe,* and a public radio show, *Travel with Rick Steves.* My website, www.ricksteves.com, offers free travel information, a forum for travelers' comments, guidebook updates, my travel blog, an online travel store, and information on European rail passes and our tours of Europe. If you're bringing a mobile device, my free Rick Steves Audio Europe app features dozens of self-guided audio tours of the top sights in Europe—including sights in Rome, Florence, Venice, Milan, Naples, Pompeii, Siena, and Assisi—plus radio shows and travel interviews about Italy. You can get Rick Steves Audio Europe via Apple's App Store, Google Play, or the Amazon Appstore. For more information, see www. ricksteves.com/audioeurope.

Additional Resources

Tourist Information: www.italia.it
Passports and Red Tape: www.travel.state.gov
Packing List: www.ricksteves.com/packing
Travel Insurance: www.ricksteves.com/insurance
Cheap Flights: www.kayak.com or www.google.com/flights
Airplane Carry-on Restrictions: www.tsa.gov/travelers
Updates for This Book: www.ricksteves.com/update

How Was Your Trip?

To share your tips, concerns, and discoveries after using this book, please fill out the survey at www.ricksteves.com/feedback. Thanks in advance—it helps a lot.

Italian Survival Phrases

English	Italian	Pronunciation
Good day.	*Buon giorno.*	bwohn **jor**-noh
Do you speak English?	*Parla inglese?*	**par**-lah een-**gleh**-zay
Yes. / No.	*Sì. / No.*	see / noh
I (don't) understand.	*(Non) capisco.*	(nohn) kah-**pees**-koh
Please.	*Per favore.*	pehr fah-**voh**-ray
Thank you.	*Grazie.*	**graht**-see-ay
You're welcome.	*Prego.*	**preh**-go
I'm sorry.	*Mi dispiace.*	mee dee-spee-**ah**-chay
Excuse me.	*Mi scusi.*	mee **skoo**-zee
(No) problem.	*(Non) c'è problema.*	(nohn) cheh proh-**bleh**-mah
Good.	*Va bene.*	vah **beh**-nay
Goodbye.	*Arrivederci.*	ah-ree-veh-**dehr**-chee
one / two	*uno / due*	**oo**-noh / **doo**-ay
three / four	*tre / quattro*	tray / **kwah**-troh
five / six	*cinque / sei*	**cheeng**-kway / **seh**-ee
seven / eight	*sette / otto*	**seh**-tay / **oh**-toh
nine / ten	*nove / dieci*	**noh**-vay / dee-**ay**-chee
How much is it?	*Quanto costa?*	**kwahn**-toh **koh**-stah
Write it?	*Me lo scrive?*	may loh **skree**-vay
Is it free?	*È gratis?*	eh **grah**-tees
Is it included?	*È incluso?*	eh een-**kloo**-zoh
Where can I buy / find...?	*Dove posso comprare / trovare...?*	**doh**-vay poh-soh kohm-**prah**-ray / troh-**vah**-ray
I'd like / We'd like...	*Vorrei / Vorremmo...*	voh-**reh**-ee / voh-**reh**-moh
...a room.	*...una camera.*	**oo**-nah **kah**-meh-rah
...a ticket to ____.	*...un biglietto per ____.*	oon beel-**yeh**-toh pehr ____
Is it possible?	*È possibile?*	eh poh-**see**-bee-lay
Where is...?	*Dov'è...?*	doh-**veh**
...the train station	*...la stazione*	lah staht-see-**oh**-nay
...the bus station	*...la stazione degli autobus*	lah staht-see-**oh**-nay **dehl**-yee ow-toh-boos
...tourist information	*...informazioni per turisti*	een-for-maht-see-**oh**-nee pehr too-**ree**-stee
...the toilet	*...la toilette*	lah twah-**leh**-tay
men	*uomini / signori*	**woh**-mee-nee / seen-**yoh**-ree
women	*donne / signore*	**doh**-nay / seen-**yoh**-ray
left / right	*sinistra / destra*	see-**nee**-strah / **deh**-strah
straight	*sempre dritto*	**sehm**-pray **dree**-toh
What time does this open / close?	*A che ora apre / chiude?*	ah kay **oh**-rah ah-**pray** / kee-**oo**-day
At what time?	*A che ora?*	ah kay **oh**-rah
Just a moment.	*Un momento.*	oon moh-**mehn**-toh
now / soon / later	*adesso / presto / tardi*	ah-**deh**-soh / **preh**-stoh / **tar**-dee
today / tomorrow	*oggi / domani*	**oh**-jee / doh-**mah**-nee

In an Italian Restaurant

English	Italian	Pronunciation
I'd like...	Vorrei...	voh-**reh**-ee
We'd like...	Vorremmo...	vor-**reh**-moh
...to reserve...	...prenotare...	preh-noh-**tah**-ray
...a table for one / two.	...un tavolo per uno / due.	oon tah-voh-loh pehr **oo**-noh / **doo**-ay
Is this seat free?	È libero questo posto?	eh **lee**-beh-roh **kweh**-stoh poh-stoh
The menu (in English), please.	Il menù (in inglese), per favore.	eel meh-**noo** (een een-**gleh**-zay) pehr fah-**voh**-ray
service (not) included	servizio (non) incluso	sehr-**veet**-see-oh (nohn) een-**kloo**-zoh
cover charge	pane e coperto	**pah**-nay ay koh-**pehr**-toh
to go	da portar via	dah **por**-tar **vee**-ah
with / without	con / senza	kohn / **sehnt**-sah
and / or	e / o	ay / oh
menu (of the day)	menù (del giorno)	meh-**noo** (dehl **jor**-noh)
specialty of the house	specialità della casa	speh-chah-lee-**tah deh**-lah **kah**-zah
first course (pasta, soup)	primo piatto	**pree**-moh pee-**ah**-toh
main course (meat, fish)	secondo piatto	seh-**kohn**-doh pee-**ah**-toh
side dishes	contorni	kohn-**tor**-nee
bread	pane	**pah**-nay
cheese	formaggio	for-**mah**-joh
sandwich	panino	pah-**nee**-noh
soup	zuppa	**tsoo**-pah
salad	insalata	een-sah-**lah**-tah
meat	carne	**kar**-nay
chicken	pollo	**poh**-loh
fish	pesce	**peh**-shay
seafood	frutti di mare	**froo**-tee dee **mah**-ray
fruit / vegetables	frutta / legumi	**froo**-tah / lay-**goo**-mee
dessert	dolce	**dohl**-chay
tap water	acqua del rubinetto	**ah**-kwah dehl roo-bee-**neh**-toh
mineral water	acqua minerale	**ah**-kwah mee-neh-**rah**-lay
milk	latte	**lah**-tay
(orange) juice	succo (d'arancia)	**soo**-koh (dah-**rahn**-chah)
coffee / tea	caffè / tè	kah-**feh** / teh
wine	vino	**vee**-noh
red / white	rosso / bianco	**roh**-soh / bee-**ahn**-koh
glass / bottle	bicchiere / bottiglia	bee-kee-**eh**-ray / boh-**teel**-yah
beer	birra	**bee**-rah
Cheers!	Cin cin!	cheen cheen
More. / Another.	Di più. / Un altro.	dee pew / oon **ahl**-troh
The same.	Lo stesso.	loh **steh**-soh
The bill, please.	Il conto, per favore.	eel **kohn**-toh pehr fah-**voh**-ray
Do you accept credit cards?	Accettate carte di credito?	ah-cheh-**tah**-tay **kar**-tay dee **kreh**-dee-toh
tip	mancia	**mahn**-chah
Delicious!	Delizioso!	day-leet-see-**oh**-zoh

For more user-friendly Italian phrases, check out *Rick Steves' Italian Phrase Book & Dictionary* or *Rick Steves' French, Italian, & German Phrase Book*.

INDEX

Our website enhances this book and turns

Explore Europe

At ricksteves.com you can browse through thousands of articles, videos, photos and radio interviews, plus find a wealth of money-saving travel tips for planning your dream trip. And with our mobile-friendly website, you can easily access all this great travel information anywhere you go.

TV Shows

Preview the places you'll visit by watching entire half-hour episodes of Rick Steves' Europe (choose from all 100 shows) on-demand, for free.

ricksteves.com

your travel dreams into affordable reality

Radio Interviews

Enjoy ready access to Rick's vast library of radio interviews covering travel

tips and cultural insights that relate specifically to your Europe travel plans.

Travel Forums

Learn, ask, share! Our online community of savvy travelers is a great resource for first-time travelers to Europe, as well as seasoned pros. You'll find forums on each country, plus travel tips and restaurant/hotel reviews. You can even ask one of our well-traveled staff to chime in with an opinion.

Travel News

Subscribe to our free Travel News e-newsletter, and get monthly updates from Rick on what's happening in Europe.

Audio Europe™

Rick's Free Travel App

Get your FREE **Rick Steves Audio Europe**™ app to enjoy...

- Dozens of self-guided tours of Europe's top museums, sights and historic walks
- Hundreds of tracks filled with cultural insights and sightseeing tips from Rick's radio interviews
- All organized into handy geographic playlists
- For Apple and Android

With Rick whispering in your ear, Europe gets even better.

Find out more at ricksteves.com

Pack Light and Right

Gear up for your next adventure at ricksteves.com

Light Luggage

Pack light and right with Rick Steves' affordable, custom-designed rolling carry-on bags, backpacks, day packs and shoulder bags.

Accessories

From packing cubes to moneybelts and beyond, Rick has personally selected the travel goodies that will help your trip go smoother.

Experience maximum Europe

Save time and energy

This guidebook is your independent-travel toolkit. But for all it delivers, it's still up to you to devote the time and energy it takes to manage the preparation and logistics that are essential for a happy trip. If that's a hassle, there's a solution.

Rick Steves Tours

A Rick Steves tour takes you to Europe's most interesting places with great

great tours, too!

with minimum stress

guides and small groups of 28 or less. We follow Rick's favorite itineraries, ride in comfy buses, stay in family-run hotels, and bring you intimately close to the Europe you've traveled so far to see. Most importantly, we take away the logistical headaches so you can focus on the fun.

travelers—nearly half of them repeat customers— along with us on four dozen different itineraries, from Ireland to Italy to Athens. Is a Rick Steves tour the right fit for your travel dreams? Find out at ricksteves.com, where you can also request Rick's latest tour catalog. Europe is best experienced with happy travel partners. We hope you can join us.

Join the fun
This year we'll take thousands of free-spirited

See our itineraries at ricksteves.com

A Guide for Every Trip

BEST OF GUIDES

Full color easy-to-scan format, focusing on Europe's most popular destinations and sights.

Best of France
Best of Germany
Best of England
Best of Europe
Best of Ireland
Best of Italy
Best of Spain

COMPREHENSIVE GUIDES

City, country, and regional guides with detailed coverage for a multi-week trip exploring the most iconic sights and venturing off the beaten track.

Amsterdam & the Netherlands
Barcelona
Belgium: Bruges, Brussels,
   Antwerp & Ghent
Berlin
Budapest
Croatia & Slovenia
Eastern Europe
England
Florence & Tuscany
France
Germany
Great Britain
Greece: Athens & the Peloponnese
Iceland
Ireland
Istanbul
Italy
London
Paris
Portugal
Prague & the Czech Republic
Provence & the French Riviera
Rome
Scandinavia
Scotland
Spain
Switzerland
Venice
Vienna, Salzburg & Tirol

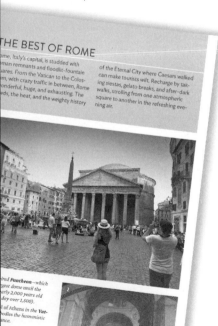

THE BEST OF ROME

ome, Italy's capital, is studded with
oman remnants and floodlit-fountain
ares. From the Vatican to the Colos-
m, with crazy traffic in between, Rome
onderful, huge, and exhausting. The
ds, the heat, and the weighty history

of the Eternal City where Caesars walked
can make tourists wilt. Recharge by taking siestas, gelato breaks, and after-dark
walks, strolling from one atmospheric
square to another in the refreshing evening air.

Rick Steves guidebooks are published by Avalon Travel,
an imprint of Perseus Books, a Hachette Book Group company.

POCKET GUIDES

Compact, full color city guides with the essentials for shorter trips.

Amsterdam
Athens
Barcelona
Florence
Italy's Cinque Terre
London
Munich & Salzburg

Paris
Prague
Rome
Venice
Vienna

SNAPSHOT GUIDES

Focused single-destination coverage.

Basque Country: Spain & France
Copenhagen & the Best of Denmark
Dublin
Dubrovnik
Edinburgh
Hill Towns of Central Italy
Krakow, Warsaw & Gdansk
Lisbon
Loire Valley
Madrid & Toledo
Milan & the Italian Lakes District
Naples & the Amalfi Coast
Northern Ireland
Normandy
Norway
Reykjavik
Sevilla, Granada & Southern Spain
St. Petersburg, Helsinki & Tallinn
Stockholm

CRUISE PORTS GUIDES

Reference for cruise ports of call.

Mediterranean Cruise Ports
Northern European Cruise Ports

Complete your library with...

TRAVEL SKILLS & CULTURE

Study up on travel skills and gain insight on history and culture.

Europe 101
European Christmas
European Easter
European Festivals
Europe Through the Back Door
Postcards from Europe
Travel as a Political Act

PHRASE BOOKS & DICTIONARIES

French
French, Italian & German
German
Italian
Portuguese
Spanish

PLANNING MAPS

Britain, Ireland & London
Europe
France & Paris
Germany, Austria & Switzerland
Ireland
Italy
Spain & Portugal

Avalon Travel
Hachette Book Group
1700 Fourth Street
Berkeley, CA 94710

Text © 2018 by Rick Steves' Europe, Inc. All rights reserved.
Maps © 2018 by Rick Steves' Europe, Inc. All rights reserved.
Printed in Canada by Friesens
First printing January 2018

Third Edition
ISBN 978-1-63121-677-0

For the latest on Rick's lectures, guidebooks, tours, public radio show, and public television series, contact Rick Steves' Europe, Inc., 130 Fourth Avenue North, Edmonds, WA 98020, tel. 425/771-8303, www.ricksteves.com, rick@ricksteves.com.

Rick Steves' Europe
Managing Editor: Jennifer Madison Davis
Special Publications Manager: Risa Laib
Assistant Managing Editor: Cathy Lu
Editors: Glenn Eriksen, Tom Griffin, Katherine Gustafson, Mary Keils, Suzanne Kotz, Rosie Leutzinger, Carrie Shepherd
Editorial & Production Assistant: Jessica Shaw
Editorial Intern: Claire Connor
Researchers: Virginia Agostinelli, Ben Cameron, Sarah Murdoch
Contributor: Gene Openshaw
Graphic Content Director: Sandra Hundacker
Maps & Graphics: David C. Hoerlein, Lauren Mills, Mary Rostad

Avalon Travel
Senior Editor and Series Manager: Madhu Prasher
Editor: Jamie Andrade
Associate Editor: Sierra Machado
Copy Editor: Maggie Ryan
Proofreaders: Patrick Collins, Suzie Nasol, Patty Mon
Indexer: Stephen Callahan
Production and Typesetting: Krista Anderson, Rue Flaherty, Jane Musser
Cover Design: Kimberly Glyder Design
Maps & Graphics: Kat Bennett

Photo Credits
Front Cover: © Buena Vista Images/Getty
Title Page: Piazza dei Signori, Padu © Dominic Arizona Bonuccelli
Additional Photography: Sistine Chapel, p. 887 © Erich Lessing/Art Resources, NY; Dominic Arizona Bonuccelli, Ben Cameron, Trish Feaster, Simon Griffith, Jennifer Hauseman, Cameron Hewitt, David C. Hoerlein, Suzanne Kotz, Gene Openshaw, Michael Potter, Robyn Stencil, Rick Steves, Bruce VanDeventer, Laura VanDeventer, Ian Watson, Wikimedia Commons (PD-Art/PD-US). (Photos are used by permission and are the property of the original copyright owners.)

ABOUT THE AUTHOR

RICK STEVES

 Since 1973, Rick has spent about four months a year exploring Europe. His mission: to empower Americans to have European trips that are fun, affordable, and culturally broadening. Rick produces a best-selling guidebook series, a public television series, and a public radio show, and organizes small-group tours that take over 20,000 travelers to Europe annually. He does all of this with the help of a hardworking, well-traveled staff of 100 at Rick Steves' Europe in Edmonds, Washington, near Seattle. When not on the road, Rick is active in his church and with advocacy groups focused on economic justice, drug policy reform, and ending hunger. To recharge, Rick plays piano, relaxes at his family cabin in the Cascade Mountains, and spends time with his partner Trish, son Andy, and daughter Jackie. Find out more about Rick at www.ricksteves.com and on Facebook.

Want More Italy?
Maximize the experience with Rick Steves as your guide

Guidebooks
Venice, Florence, and Rome guides make side-trips smooth and affordable

Phrase Books
Rely on Rick's Italian Phrase Book and Dictionary

Rick's DVDs
Preview where you're going with 15 shows on Italy

Free! Rick's Audio Europe™ App
Get free audio tours for Italy's top sights

Small-Group Tours
Rick offers a dozen great itineraries through Italy

For all the details, visit ricksteves.com